I0016824

Raising Young Coders

A Parent's Guide to Teaching Programming at Home

Cassandra Chin

Apress®

Raising Young Coders: A Parent's Guide to Teaching Programming at Home

Cassandra Chin
Belmont, CA, USA

ISBN-13 (pbk): 979-8-8688-1392-4 ISBN-13 (electronic): 979-8-8688-1393-1
https://doi.org/10.1007/979-8-8688-1393-1

Managing Director, Apress Media LLC: Welmoed Spahr
Acquisitions Editor: Melissa Duffy
Desk Editor: James Markham
Editorial Project Manager: Gryffin Winkler

Cover designed by eStudioCalamar

Distributed to the book trade worldwide by Springer Science+Business Media New York, 1 New York Plaza, Suite 4600, New York, NY 10004-1562, USA. Phone 1-800-SPRINGER, fax (201) 348-4505, e-mail orders-ny@springer-sbm.com, or visit www.springeronline.com. Apress Media, LLC is a California LLC and the sole member (owner) is Springer Science + Business Media Finance Inc (SSBM Finance Inc). SSBM Finance Inc is a **Delaware** corporation.

For information on translations, please e-mail booktranslations@springernature.com; for reprint, paperback, or audio rights, please e-mail bookpermissions@springernature.com.

Apress titles may be purchased in bulk for academic, corporate, or promotional use. eBook versions and licenses are also available for most titles. For more information, reference our Print and eBook Bulk Sales web page at http://www.apress.com/bulk-sales.

Any source code or other supplementary material referenced by the author in this book is available to readers on GitHub. For more detailed information, please visit https://www.apress.com/gp/services/source-code.

If disposing of this product, please recycle the paper

To my Dad who inspired me to share my love of technology with kids and parents.

Table of Contents

About the Author

 **Cassandra Chin** is a keynote speaker, book author, video podcast host, and long-time children's workshop instructor. Since her teenage years, she has been sharing her passion for coding with children, leading workshops at international events such as Devoxx4Kids, KidzMash, JFokus4Kids, and CNCF Kids Day. Her extensive experience has equipped her with effective strategies to inspire young learners to discover programming for fun. In 2024, Cassandra published *Phippy's AI Friend: Story and Workshop for Kids and Parents*, a resource designed to assist parents in introducing technology to their children. Additionally, she hosts and produces a podcast where she interviews speakers, educators, and tech professionals in the community to discuss topics related to education for children and young adults.

LinkedIn: `https://www.linkedin.com/in/cassandra-chin-developer`

Acknowledgments

When I was in elementary school, I would attend kids workshops with my friends as a fun weekend activity. I saw ways that the content could be improved and made more fun and engaging, so I wanted to try teaching my own workshop. It was a little unusual that most of the kids I taught were either the same age or a little older than me, but they respected me more than an adult and gave me their full attention. I want to thank John Kostaras, Heinz Kabutz, and Kirk Pepperdine who run kids workshops at the JCrete Unconference and let me teach there. I would also like to thank Mattias Karlsson and Helena Hjertén who organize the Jfokus conference in Stockholm and have supported my passion for teaching since I was little. Thanks also to the SF Bay Area Devoxx4Kids team led by Arun Gupta and Kevin Nilson where I have taught a lot of kids workshops. And finally, Margo Davis who organized JavaOne and JavaOne4Kids.

After teaching kids workshops for many years, I realized it would be more impactful to motivate the adults to want to teach their kids technology, so I wanted to give a conference session about it. Most speakers are old and accomplished tech geeks, which meant I didn't fit the norm; however, I had a surprising amount of public speaking experience and content from teaching kids workshops. I am greatly thankful to Vincent Meyers who organizes Devnexus and gave me my first keynote opportunity and Badr El Houari who runs Devoxx Morocco and let me keynote there.

I wrote my first book, *Phippy's AI Friend*, which is a picture book that includes a kids workshop activity. I wanted to create a book which could be enjoyed by both technical and nontechnical families and inspire them to enjoy technology. This has also taught me that writing a book for something I am passionate about can be a lot of fun. Writing *Phippy's AI Friend* has given me a lot of opportunities to meet new people and has inspired me to write this book, *Raising Young Coders*. I want to thank Chris Aniszczyk for supporting the book writing from the CNCF and Romain Thérenty, the illustrator and my new friend.

I would also like to thank Melissa Duffy, the acquisitions editor for Apress. I met her after my Devnexus keynote, and she has been supportive of the book proposal and writing process. At every step, she put in extra effort to making *Raising Young Coders* possible, and I know she is as excited as I am that this book is being published as a resource for parents to inspire their kids to love technology.

A big thanks to Hippie Hacker who is an amazing kids' mentor and helped tech review this book.

CHAPTER 1

Why Learning Tech Is Important for Kids

This book teaches you how to inspire your kids to enjoy and pursue technology. Many books try to make your kid an expert in programming, but that is not the right approach. Kids should be inspired and see that technology is not that difficult and a lot of fun, so they will want to do more technology in the future.

Currently, I am a young woman majoring in computer science, so I have a lot of recent experience growing up with technology and seeing how other kids approach it. I grew up in a house surrounded by technology like computers, Raspberry Pis, and videogames, and I saw how that influenced my passion for it. I had coding books and resources available to me, but I found them boring, so they mostly collected dust. If I had been forced to learn a programming language at a young age, I may not have developed the same passion I have for technology today. After I saw how much fun technology was, I decided to learn a programming language much later in high school. It is best to show kids the creative and fun parts of technology first so that they will gain an interest in it.

I also attended kids workshops with my friends and started teaching workshops very early on at the age of 14 and haven't stopped since. I have taught and seen a lot of workshops, so I know what content kids enjoy and what content will cause their attention to go elsewhere. Many kids and parents ask how they can continue the workshop at home, which lets me know that they have been inspired to go further with technology.

C. Chin, *Raising Young Coders*, https://doi.org/10.1007/979-8-8688-1393-1_1

I have put together my experiences and recommendations in this book in hopes that I can inspire more kids and girls to enjoy and pursue technology. Technology is not as hard as it looks and actually is a lot of fun and has an infinite potential for the future. Technology is not limited to just computer science. There is technology behind education systems, healthcare, finance, mobile apps, and almost every field. Technology is not just about computers, and it is the starting point for a variety of different careers.

Inspire, Don't Push

Inspiring kids to be interested in technology in a fun way is important so that they will be passionate about it in the future. The heart of programming is creativity and problem-solving. Many textbooks and beginner programming courses get this wrong because they will start teaching your kids with a programming language like Python which is too complicated for young learners. It is similar to learning a new world language in hopes you can write a story with it one day. Starting with an age-appropriate technology like the projects in this book will let your kids create something and have fun. If your kids have fun doing technology, then they will want to do more of it in the future.

It is important to give your kids a lot of opportunities to try different activities to see what they enjoy. If you have girls, you may limit them to gender stereotype activities like dancing, cooking, or making bracelets. I tried a variety of these activities when I was little, but I also tried technology. I ended up enjoying technology the most because I like creating things that move on video screens or seeing LEDs light up. It is important to give your kids the opportunity to try lots of different activities so that they know what they enjoy. If you don't let your kids try the technology, then they are missing out on something they could be passionate about.

There are a lot of ways you can introduce technology to your kids in a fun way. When I was little, I was given a desktop computer that had to be built with parts. The computer had a case and internal parts like the motherboard, graphics processing unit, memory, and more. I let my dad do the boring part which was reading the manual, and I helped to assemble the components and screw in the parts. This is a great way to learn computer science early on because it helps you to understand what makes up a computer and see it with your own eyes. It is more exciting to learn why the computer has both an SSD and RAM when you see the physical parts and memory capacity written on the sticks. The issue with building a computer with your kid is computers are expensive, and it can easily cost $1000 and up to buy all the parts. Raspberry Pis are a great alternative to building your own computer because they are much more affordable at only $35.

Raspberry Pis Should Be Every Kid's First Computer

The Raspberry Pi is best described as a minicomputer. It is a green board about the size of your hand with lots of components soldered to it. Most of the kids workshops I have taught before were about how to use the Raspberry Pi. It is a great tool for education because it works like a computer, and I have the kids code and run the games that they code. The Raspberry Pi itself is also kid-friendly because it is very sturdy. I have traveled with a set of 16 to many international conferences, and it is always the cables that break before the Raspberry Pis.

The Raspberry Pi was created by the Raspberry Pi Foundation with the idea that computers should be both powerful enough and affordable so that they can be used for education. They released their first Raspberry Pi in 2012 which also happens to be shortly after the smartphone boom. Smartphones and tablets take away from technology learning because the apps just work magically, and it is impossible for kids to write their own apps. You need a desktop computer and developer license to code for your device, which is out of reach for kids. The Raspberry Pi bridges the gap between a very expensive computer and a smartphone, making it possible to learn coding affordably and in an educational environment.

The Raspberry Pi is my favorite computer to use when I am teaching kids workshops. I taught a Raspberry Pi workshop for Black Girls Code as seen in Figure 1-1. Many of the girls who attended my workshop didn't have computers at home, so they got to experience their first computer by plugging wires into their Raspberry Pi and using a keyboard to code. The parents and workshop organizers were interested to know what a Raspberry Pi can do and how easy it is to obtain one. Since Raspberry Pis are very powerful and affordable, they make a great computer for kids of any background to learn technology.

Figure 1-1. *A pair of girls learning technology for the first time using the Raspberry Pi*

I have seen a lot of Raspberry Pis globally in places you wouldn't expect. I visited a tea farm in Taiwan, and they had Raspberry Pis in their fields with sensors to measure temperature and humidity. I have also seen Pis used to emulate old video game consoles under TVs. Raspberry Pis are very affordable and can be bought in almost any country. It can be a little confusing to know where to buy one, but the easiest way is to visit the Raspberry Pi site and find the model of Raspberry Pi you want. The Raspberry Pi site doesn't directly sell any Raspberry Pis, but they will help redirect you to one of their approved reseller websites. They have different websites for each country, so you should be able to find the website which is best for you.

My first Raspberry Pi was a Raspberry Pi 2. I used it with my dad, and he taught me how to launch a small pixel art sheep game using the Nano editor. I learned how to modify the colors of the sheep in code and also to create an infinite number of sheep to fill the screen, which was a lot of fun. Even though this was almost ten years ago, the Raspberry Pi 2 was very powerful, and I saw it being used for many hobby projects like controlling robots! Now there are even more powerful Raspberry Pi models available at a very affordable price.

Next time you are thinking about what to buy your kids for their birthday or Christmas, buy them a Raspberry Pi instead of their usual toys and video games. The Raspberry Pi will get you through the exercises in Chapter 4, and it will help you and your kids to continue to learn with other Raspberry Pi community projects.

Not All Screen Time Is Bad

Screen time limits are used to limit the amount of time kids spend on their devices. Within the past few years, screen time limits have become universal and are available on almost every device and system, including

Mac, Windows, video game consoles, and more. Screen time limits are great for limiting your child's use of passive activities like YouTube and games, but they also will prohibit your child from spending time on educational software like Scratch after time is up. Not all screen time is equal, so it can help to break your child's screen time into different categories:

- Passive: This includes YouTube, social media, and reading blogs where there is no activity or input involved.

- Active: These are activities like texting friends and family, playing games, and digitally drawing. All of these activities require you to think and do something.

- Learning: Examples of this are using Scratch, Hour of Code, Greenfoot, or any activity where you are learning or creating something.

It has become common for kids to be given devices because it is effective at occupying their time. I have a much younger sister, and she is usually on her phone watching YouTube or playing games on her computer. But we put screen time limits on her devices, and they help her to refocus herself to do her homework or find other hobbies. With how addicting watching YouTube or social media can be, screen time limits are most parent's best friend.

The problem with strictly limiting screen time is not all screen time is equal. *Passive* screen time is what most kids will default to, and it is not a good use of their time. Too much of it can even be worse for their mental health. *Active* screen time is not as harmful and can be a good hobby. However, we want our kids to use their screen time for *Learning* because it is active learning that will teach them coding concepts, and we want our kids to gain a passion for technology.

The best way to get your kids excited about screen time in the *Learning* category is by doing the projects in this book with them. The projects in this book will show your kids that technology isn't as hard as it looks and is actually a lot of fun. Kids will also enjoy the personal time that you spend with them when they are doing the projects with you. The projects are labeled by recommended age in future chapters.

With a strict screen time limit with a set number of hours, kids will feel punished for spending their time doing *Learning* activities because that will eat into their YouTube time. To solve this, most built-in screen time applications will let you decide which applications or websites kids are allowed to use after their time is up. This means that you can whitelist the educational Scratch website so that after screen time is done, kids can still use their devices but only go to the Scratch website. This encourages kids to have fun with learning technology without feeling like they lost time for their hobbies. Each screen time application is a little different, but they all have settings that can help manage your kids' time and encourage technology learning.

Diversity Starts Young – Don't Leave Your Daughters Out

I recently went to an arts and crafts store to look for gamer wall decor as seen in Figure 1-2. However, the colors they chose for the wall decor were stereotypical muted colors for boys. Some of the wall decor states, "BOYS ONLY" and "NO GIRLS ALLOWED," which reinforces gender biases. It is important that we take a step back and look at what jokes we are making so that we don't unintentionally discourage our girls from enjoying tech.

Figure 1-2. *Wall decor targeted at gamers sold at a large arts and crafts store*

Getting your young girls interested in technology is important because it not only improves diversity but also gives them the potential to have fun with tech. Currently, technology jobs and computer science jobs have a higher ratio of men to women. But technology is moving forward at a very rapid pace with new advancements like artificial intelligence, and we don't want our girls left behind.

My Experience Teaching Kids Workshops

Computer science biases and technology being perceived as a guy thing starts at a really young age. I have taught kids Raspberry Pi workshops in many parts of the world. In these classes, I teach a class of about 20 kids, and they learn some light coding and wiring. This is important because I have noticed a trend in the gender diversity of the kids I teach. I found that kids I teach in the Bay Area are predominantly boys, while kids I teach in places like Europe or even Greece and Morocco have a more balanced gender ratio. This shows that even though places like Silicon Valley are the center of tech, they may not be doing the best in working to improve gender diversity.

Figure 1-3. *This photo was taken when I taught a kids workshop at the Google headquarters*

I taught a kids workshop at the Google headquarters before as seen in Figure 1-3. At this weekend event, eager tech parents brought in their kids because they wanted them to get a head start in tech. I had a class of about ten kids; there was one girl, one parent, and the rest of them were boys. The workshop I taught was a Raspberry Pi workshop where kids use a small underpowered computer to run an 8-bit Pokemon game, and it is their job to go into the source code and write a single line of code. The kids sitting at the front of the classroom were very familiar with the device and had done a lot of gaming before, so they were catching all the Pokemon on screen before I got the class to that point.

More recently, I went to Morocco for a developer conference, and they were happy to help host a kids workshop. They connected with local schools and helped to arrange buses to get the kids to the conference venue and back. The kids that were brought in weren't all the same age, but the ratio between boys and girls was even. I also taught the same Raspberry Pi workshop here, and for many of the kids, it was their first time using a keyboard. I find moments like this very meaningful because all the kids who came to this workshop will go home thinking that technology is not just a boy's thing, but anyone can do it.

I find it surprising that high-tech areas like the Bay Area have the most issues with getting young girls interested in computer science. These areas have the most available resources like workshops, computer science programs, and STEM activities, but currently, most parents miss this opportunity and choose to only sign up their boys. I am fortunate that I had the opportunity to attend a tech workshop when I was little because that let me choose my own career path with computer science as an option. I strongly advise that if you have or know girls, give them this opportunity as well.

The Current Lack of Women in Software Engineering

Your kids don't deserve to be held back by gendered stereotypes. In the early days of computing, women were equally involved in developing early computers. But with the introduction of home computers, a bias was created where parents would buy a computer and give it to their son rather than their daughter. Fast forward to today and technology is one of the fastest-growing industries, but the industry still has a disproportionate ratio of female software developers. With technologies like artificial intelligence taking off now, who would want their child to be left behind just because of a dated gender stereotype?

Currently, many software companies still have a disproportionate ratio of software engineering women compared to men. We can see in Figure 1-4 that companies like Dropbox have a lot of software engineers, but only 10.9% are women. Only a few companies even make it close to the 50% line where there is an equal number of male and female software engineers. This is today's problem, and we don't want our kids to face the same problem when they grow up. You can help to increase diversity in technology by introducing your girls to technology or sharing this book with friends who have girls.

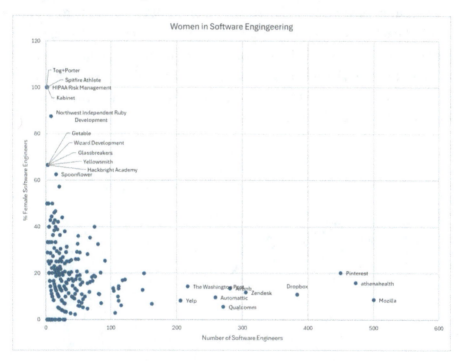

Figure 1-4. *A graph that shows the percentage of female software engineers in various companies*

It is important to introduce computers and technology to your girls while they are young. Girls who have never touched a computer or done much with tech before will underestimate their ability to be good at it and stray away from it. It is easy to feel like you can't be good at something if you have never tried it before. It is our job as parents to show our girls computers and technology early on so that they can gain the confidence that technology is something they have done before and can do more of.

Gender Stereotypes by Age

Gender stereotypes that computer science favors boys are not only found in the parents but also in the kids themselves. In a research paper in 2021, a study was conducted to survey students of various age groups and ethnical backgrounds to see if the students perceived computer science as more suited for boys or girls. In Figure 1-5, we have a graph that shows how students thought about computer science. The x-axis goes up by grade, and the y-axis shows the kids' interest in computer science where higher numbers show higher interest.

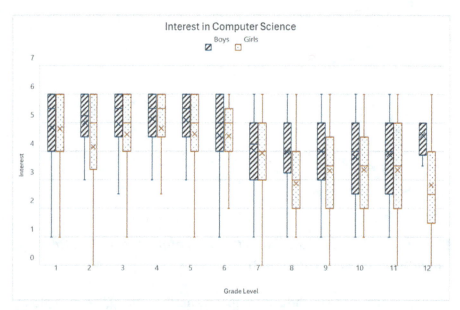

Figure 1-5. *This box and whisker graph shows boys' and girls' interest in computer science at different grade levels*

It is important that we introduce our girls to technology the same way we would with our boys. In this survey, the girls think they are less interested in computer science when compared to the boys. In the graph, the boxes representing the girls sit a little lower than the boys' boxes. Girls are equally capable of having fun with technology and being good at it. The problem is that girls haven't had the opportunity to try technology, so they wouldn't know if they were interested in it or not. Giving your girls the opportunity to try technology can make a difference, and they may come to love it.

The best time to get your kids started in computer science is when they are young, which means sooner is better. The students in grades 1–5 answered more positively about being interested in technology, while the older kids showed less interest. Kids are most willing to try new things when they are young, so the best time to introduce them to technology is as early as possible. Kids are also less influenced by gender stereotypes when they are younger, so it is also a good opportunity to show your girls that technology can be fun. Even if your kids are a little older, it is never too late to introduce them to technology, and the best time to start is now.

How Schools Approach Computer Science

What do you think of first when you hear the terminology "STEM"? This popular term stands for science, technology, engineering, and mathematics, and it puts all these subjects under the same umbrella. Most of the time, we think of STEM activities as something that only smart kids are good at, and we see a lot of this reinforced in kids' cartoons, branding for summer camps, projects, and more. Schools will often reinforce that technology is for smart kids by overusing the STEM acronym for extracurricular activities or requiring students to take math classes as a prerequisite to computer science programs.

Math and Technology Are Not the Same

We commonly think that if a kid is good at math in school, then they should be good at computer science. All schools require kids to take math, so we commonly use this as a baseline to decide if a kid would be good at computer science. The term "STEM" also puts both technology and math in the same category. If I had to enjoy math to enjoy computer science, then I would have never been willing to try it.

Math is definitely not the prerequisite to computer science. A survey was conducted on high school students to see what their attitude was toward each course, whether they had taken it or not. In Figure 1-6, we have a graph that shows the percentage of students who like each course. We can see that math is the lowest with not a lot of students liking it. Computer science and engineering has almost double the number of students who enjoy it when compared to math. Even if we assumed that all kids who like math will like computer science (which is not true), then they would still be missing out on computer science about half the time. Computer science is its own subject and shouldn't be confused with math.

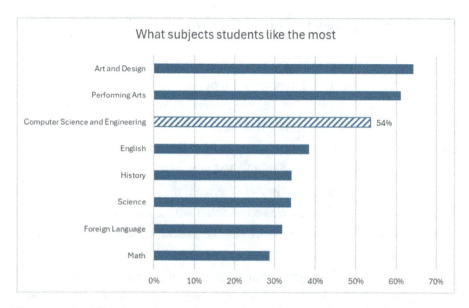

Figure 1-6. *This bar chart shows what school subjects kids enjoy the most*

Your kids do not have to be good at math to do good at computer science. When I was in high school, I didn't consider myself an A+ math student, and math was my least favorite subject. At the time, I was also taking my school's computer science class. I found that the class had a higher focus on creativity and problem-solving like how you can solve a problem with multiple different approaches.

You should expose your kids to technology in fun ways that don't involve heavy math like sending them to workshops, playing code games like Hour of Code, or trying interactive projects like the mBot. It is important to give your kids an interesting introduction to technology so that they get excited about it and will want to do more of it in the future.

You Don't Need to Be a Genius

Students do worse at computer science when they believe that only smart people can be good at it. There are a lot of biases about how coding and technology is a smart-person thing. Acronyms like STEM reinforce this bias because most of the images on the Internet for STEM portray smart kids in lab coats. Most kids have trouble associating themselves with smart kids in lab coats and will get the idea that STEM is not suited for them.

Kids will do poorly in computer science if they believe they aren't smart enough for it. A study was conducted where students were asked to read a high school newspaper that talked about how a student named Markus became a computer scientist. There were two versions of this paper, and students were given one of the two at random. The first version of the paper portrays Markus as a typical computer science genius where he started coding very young and is good at coding because of real talent. The second version of the paper portrays Markus as a student with average grades who learned how to code much later but got to where they were based on hard work. Students were asked how well they think they would do in their STEM classes this year before and after the experiment. It can be seen in Figure 1-7 that students who read the article on how Markus was a genius all answered with less confidence.

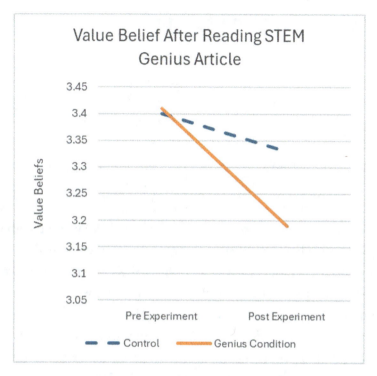

Figure 1-7. *This is a graph showing how confident students are about their STEM classes before and after reading an article characterizing STEM as a subject for geniuses*

It is our job to show our kids that technology isn't that hard and anyone can do it if they want to. Typical classroom examples of technology like STEM and posters of Einstein provide a bad example which will make your kids lose confidence. A better way to introduce kids to technology is by showing them how easy and enjoyable it is using introductory coding games like Scratch or telling stories and reading to them books about technologists who aren't perfect and more relatable to them.

Technology Outside of School

We should introduce our kids to technology without all the biases that come with it when it is taught in schools. Locally run workshops and technology programs are a great way to get your kids introduced to computer science. This is how I got into technology when my parents gave me the opportunity to attend a weekend workshop. These programs which aren't tied to the school curriculum generally have a bigger emphasis on fun projects which allow the kids to be more creative.

There are many organizations and programs designed to teach kids technology outside of school. One organization I have worked with before is Devoxx4Kids. They are a volunteer organization created in the Bay Area, and they have expanded globally. The Devoxx4Kids workshops take place during weekends and take on average two hours per workshop. Not all programs are free and volunteer driven, but that doesn't make them any worse. It is important to do your research and find what programs are available to you in your local area. Sometimes, schools will promote after-school programs related to technology or STEM. There are some summer camp programs out there too. Regardless of which program you end up on, getting your kids exposed to technology is the first step.

Getting your kids' friends involved can be the push you need to get them excited about doing more with technology. When I attended my first workshop, I went with my friend who was also excited about technology. Having her around made the workshop very enjoyable because it let us collaborate on projects outside of school. Many of the workshops we went to were also predominated by boys, so having her around made it feel like it wasn't a big deal and that we were there just to play together more outside of school. Having a friend to attend kids workshops with can make a difference for your kids.

Conclusion

It is important to inspire our kids to see that technology is fun so that they will want to do more of it in the future. There are many fun ways to make technology entertaining and affordable like using a Raspberry Pi or doing the projects in this book. It is also important that you get your daughters involved when you are teaching your kids technology. Technology is a growing industry and has the most potential, so we don't want to leave our daughters out. Schools may have computer science classes, but they often try to teach your kids a programming language, rather than showing the creative part of technology. It can be helpful to take your kids to kids workshops so that they see the fun side of technology. In the next chapter, we will look at projects you can do with your kids and which ones may be best for you.

CHAPTER 2

Early Learners

Learning about simple electrical circuits is one of the best ways to introduce technology to your kids. All the code we write and applications we run on our computers go through the computer's central processing unit. Modern processing units have billions of transistors that act as binary on and off switches. Kids can get a head start and learn about how on and off switches work on LED lights and get creative with modifying the flow of electricity to see what happens.

It is never too early for kids to start learning technology. This chapter has projects that are great for very young kids as early as the age of three. Knowing how to read and write is not a prerequisite to learning how basic circuits work. The Squishy Circuits project in this chapter will let your young kids turn their play dough creations into circuits that power LED lights. The Paper Circuits project is great for kids who enjoy arts and crafts. Their drawings will come to life with interactive LED lights powered by circuits. Learning technology early on in a fun way will inspire your kids to want to do more of it in the future.

Squishy Circuits

This project will let your kids learn how to build circuits in the most creative and hands-on way possible. Kids will get to learn with play dough experiment with the different properties of conductive dough and insulating dough. Conductive dough can be used as a medium to

© Cassandra Chin 2025
C. Chin, *Raising Young Coders*, https://doi.org/10.1007/979-8-8688-1393-1_2

let electricity flow, meaning you can create play dough sculptures with working LED lights. This project is great for young kids because they don't need to know how to read and write. Any kid can build a shape out of play dough, and you can help them bring it to life with electricity.

- Age range: 3–8 (or older if this is their first project)

- Difficulty: Beginner

- Amount of time: 1–2 hours

- Learning outcomes: Learn how circuits work hands-on, build with play dough

- Materials needed: Squishy Circuits kit (standard or deluxe kit), four AA batteries

Getting Started

For the projects in this book, you are only required to have the Squishy Circuits standard kit. The standard kit comes with LED lights, a buzzer, and red, green, blue, and white dough. The deluxe kit comes with more sensors and dough color, but we won't be using any of the extra sensors in this book, so just having the standard kit is enough.

If your child has gluten intolerance, having them play with play dough can make them sick. You can find the conductive dough and insulating dough recipes on a card in your kit or on the Squishy Circuits website. Simply substitute the flour with gluten-free one for one flour.

When you first open your Squishy Circuits kit, I recommend following the exercise in the quick start guide. It will teach you the basics of how to get an LED light to light up with your play dough. The white dough is an insulating dough that will block electricity. The colored dough is a conductive dough which lets electricity pass through it. The colored dough is perfectly interchangeable, so if you don't have a color, you can substitute it with any color except white.

Making a Pokeball

For this first project, we will be making a Pokeball with a button that lights up. This is what you will need to build it:

- Battery holder

- One LED

- Red and black conductive dough (you can substitute the black dough with a different color if you don't have it)

- White insulating dough

Making the Pokeball

To make the Pokeball, take a very large clump of red play dough and another very large clump of black play dough as seen in Figure 2-1. This will make the top and bottom halves of the Pokeball. Most of your red and black play dough jar should be empty depending on how big you want your Pokeball to be. Roll the red play dough into a sphere as round as you can by putting the dough in between your two hands and making a circular motion with them. Do the same thing to the black play dough. If the two spheres aren't the same size, you can remove some dough from one and try rolling it into a sphere again.

Figure 2-1. *Two large circular red and black play dough balls*

Slicing the Spheres in Half

Cut both of your dough balls in half with a plastic knife as seen in Figure 2-2. You can either make the cut straight down, or you can go around the sphere with your knife and score the edges. No one will see the inner face of the semisphere, so it doesn't matter how it looks. Pick your two favorite halves to use for the Pokeball. You won't need the other two halves, so you can put them back into your dough containers.

Figure 2-2. *The two dough spheres cut in half*

Building the Middle Layer

Grab the black dough half; this is the dough half you will be using for the bottom of your Pokeball. Take a small clump of white insulating dough and roll it into a sphere. Then gently shape the sphere into a pancake by smashing it in between your hands or the table. The white dough pancake should be just large enough to cover the black dough half when you set it on top. You can see what this looks like in Figure 2-3. You might be thinking that Pokeballs have white bottoms and black separator lines in the middle. But we are doing this in reverse because we need the white insulating dough to block electric current between the two semispheres.

Figure 2-3. *Black dough semicircle with a white insulating dough pancake on top*

Putting the Pokeball Halves Together

Put the red half of the Pokeball on top of the white insulating dough pancake. Make sure that the top and bottom half aren't touching anywhere as seen in Figure 2-4. You need the white insulating dough to separate the electric current between the two halves. If the two halves are touching at any point, it will short-circuit the LED light we are adding in later.

Figure 2-4. *The Pokeball mostly assembled and with a small clump of white dough for the button*

Adding the Pokeball's Button

Next, we are going to add the white button to the Pokeball as seen in Figure 2-5. Take a small clump of white dough and roll it into a sphere. Flatten it a little to get it to the size button you want. Choose the side of the Pokeball which you think looks best and place the white button on the white line, between the two halves.

Figure 2-5. *The Pokeball with the white button*

Inserting an LED Light

This next step can be a little tricky. Take an LED light of any color you choose. Notice that the LED has two wires going down, and one of them is longer than the other. Separate the two wires so it makes a slim V shape. Insert it into the Pokeball button with the longer wire facing up. The wires on the LED should be split apart wide enough that when you press it into the Pokeball, they make contact with the top red and bottom black play dough. You can see the result in Figure 2-6.

Figure 2-6. *The Pokeball with the LED light inserted*

Wiring the Pokeball

The Pokeball is almost finished. Turn the Pokeball around so you can see the back of it. Grab your battery holder and make sure it has batteries in it. There should be a red wire and a blue wire sticking out of the battery holder. Use the end with the red wire and poke a hole in the top half of the Pokeball. Do the same thing with the black wire, but poke a hole in the bottom half of the Pokeball as seen in Figure 2-7. It is safer to put the holes further away from the center to make sure they don't ever touch each other. Turn on the power on the battery holder, and your LED will light up! You have now constructed a Pokeball.

If your LED light doesn't light up, there could be a few issues. The first possibility is you inserted the LED in the wrong direction. The LED has two prongs, and one is longer than the other. Electric current has a positive and negative, so it matters which way you insert the LED. The quickest fix is to swap the red and black wires on the back of the Pokeball.

Another possibility is you could have short-circuited your electric current somewhere. If the top and bottom half of the Pokeball are touching anywhere, the electricity will take the path of least resistance and skip going through the LED light. You can also double-check your LED light. When you insert it, the prongs should be wide enough that they touch the top and bottom colored play dough on the inside. The fix would be to take the LED out and widen the prongs, then insert it again.

Figure 2-7. *The Pokeball with the red wire on top and the black wire on the bottom*

Making the Pokeball Glow

You can see the finished Pokeball in Figure 2-8. With the LED at its center, you have constructed a simple circuit where electricity flows through. The battery pack supplies the electricity and sends it down the red wire.

It sees the end of the LED touching it and goes through the LED light. Then it flows down the other side of the LED and goes through the black play dough. Eventually, it makes it back to the battery pack.

At this point, you have finished the Pokeball project. You can get creative and sketch some designs into the Pokeball, build a mini Pokémon on the side, or think of your own ideas. I definitely recommend snapping a photo of your project while the play dough is still moist. Play dough does tend to dry out after a few hours, so make sure to clean it up within the same day. In the next Squishy Circuits project, you will learn how to build slimes and electrical flow with the buzzer.

Figure 2-8. *The finished Pokeball with the glowing LED light in the center*

Friendly Slimes

For the second project, we will build three slimes and see how they interact with each other along with the buzzer and a LED light.

- Battery holder

- One red LED

- Piezoelectric buzzer

- Blue, red, green, and black conductive dough (you can substitute the black dough with a different color if you don't have it)

- White insulating dough

We are going to build three slimes for this project. Slimes can look very goofy, and you can get creative with their body and faces. There is no wrong answer when it comes to building slimes; I will be showing you how I build the slimes.

Dough for the Blue Slime

We are going to build the blue slime first. Grab a good chunk of blue play dough; this will be the slime's body. You can decide how big you want your slime, but it is easier to work with a larger play dough chunk, so you have space to add facial features later. It may also be good to save a little bit of blue play dough in case you want to use it later. I have also laid out the other play dough colors you will need to build this slime as seen in Figure 2-9. The colors are red, black, and white. If you have the basic kit, you can substitute green instead of black.

Figure 2-9. *A large clump of blue play dough for the slime's body and smaller clumps of red, black (or green), and white play dough for the slime's facial features later*

Molding the Blue Slime's Body

Take the blue play dough ball and mold it into the shape you want for your slime. I made mine with a plump body and tip at the end as shown in Figure 2-10. To make the tip, pinch one end of the play dough to make it pointy. Shape the point until you like how it looks. To make the plump body, press the dough on the table so the bottom gets flat. A good place to press is the area around the point, which will also help give your point a more defined shape. Pressing the slime on the table will help the slime stand without rolling away, and it gives it a plumper oval figure.

Figure 2-10. *The blue play dough molded to look like a slime body with a plump body and pointy end*

Building Facial Features

Next, we will be making the face of the blue slime. You can see the facial parts laid out in Figure 2-11. Roll out two small white pieces of dough, and try to make them the same size. This will be the white parts of the eyes. Flatten them a little bit to the size you want. Next, pinch two tiny pieces of black play dough. They should be very tiny and will be the pupils for your slime's eyes. If you don't have black play dough, you can use green play dough or whatever color you want your slime's pupils to be. For the mouth, take a small clump of red play dough and roll it into a sphere. Then roll it in your hands or against the table to make it long. Try to roll it evenly by rolling the center as well; it's easy to make the edges thinner. I curled the edges of my red play dough stick in to even it out.

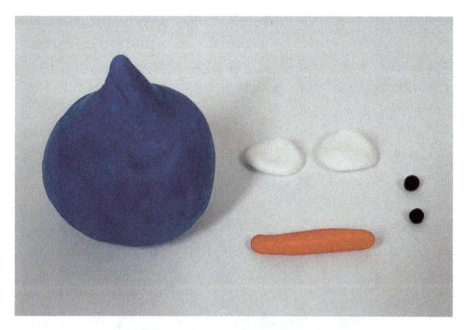

Figure 2-11. *The face parts of the slime laid out*

Giving the Slime a Face

With all the face parts of the slime laid out, we need to assemble the slime's face. The finished result can be seen in Figure 2-12. First, put the mouthpiece on the slime by curving the red play dough stick with a slight U shape. Press the play dough in, and it should stick just enough to keep hold. Next, we need to put the two eyes in place. Grab both white play dough pancakes and align them above the mouth. Holding both eyepieces at the same time makes it easier to center them relative to the mouth. When you are happy with the position, stick it to the slime and apply pressure.

Getting the pupils in is a little trickier; it is hard to get the pupils to stick to the eyes without turning the pupils into flat pancakes. I used the small ball point tool in the deluxe kit to make indentations in the center of the white play dough where you want the eyes to go. You can also use a pencil to carve out the indentations. The indentations don't need to be that deep, and they should be a little smaller than the size of your black play dough pupils. When you have finished creating your indentations, insert the black pupils into each eye and apply slight pressure. Then you have your finished blue slime!

Figure 2-12. *Completed blue slime. May resemble a slime from a certain video game...*

Building a Green Friend

Your blue slime needs a friend which can be seen in Figure 2-13. For the second slime, follow the same instructions for the blue slime but use green play dough instead of blue play dough. If you are feeling adventurous, you can pick any color except white for the body. You can also design your own facial expressions as they are just cosmetic on these basic slimes.

Figure 2-13. *The blue slime is on the left, and the new green slime is on the right*

Building the White Slime

The third slime is the trickiest to build, so I recommend following the instructions closely. We are going to build a white slime with insulating dough on the outside and conductive dough on the inside. You will need some white play dough and colored play dough as seen in Figure 2-14. Both play dough balls will be much smaller than your already-built slimes. If you imagine combining both play dough balls, it should be about the same size as your other slimes. I used green for my colored play dough ball, but the color doesn't matter so you should use whichever color you have the most of left. The colored play dough ball should be a little smaller than your white insulating dough ball.

Figure 2-14. *A colored play dough ball on the left and a slightly larger white insulating dough ball on the right*

Creating the White Slime's Body

We are going to use the white play dough to have it wrap around the colored play dough. Roll the white insulating play dough into a sphere, then flatten it into a pancake. It should be large enough to fully wrap around the colored dough ball as seen in Figure 2-15. You can place the colored dough ball in the center of the white dough ball pancake to help visualize whether your white dough will fit around. Make sure your white dough pancake is thick enough that it will completely cover the colored dough ball without stretching thin. If you think you don't have enough material, you can add more white dough to your white dough pancake and try again.

Figure 2-15. *The white insulating dough is flattened into a pancake with the colored dough sitting in the center*

Wrapping the White Dough

Wrap the white insulating dough around your colored dough ball as seen in Figure 2-16. You will want to have some excess white dough at the top so that you can shape it into a point later.

Figure 2-16. *The white insulating dough wrapped around the colored conductive dough*

Molding the White Slime into Shape

Shape the surrounding white insulating dough to make it look like a slime, similar to the other two slimes. First, close up the top where your white dough connects when you wrap it around the colored dough. You should have some excess dough here; use it to shape it and mold it into a point for the top of the slime. Be more gentle when you are shaping this slime since you don't want to accidentally expose the colored dough. Refer to Figure 2-17 to see what the shaped slime looks like.

Figure 2-17. *The finished white slime body with the colored dough on the inside*

Constructing Eyes and a Bow for the White Slime

The white slime needs a face; the facial parts can be seen in Figure 2-18. Since this slime is white, we won't be using white dough for the eyes this time. For the eyes, grab two small pieces of black dough and roll each one into a sphere. Then gently roll in one direction to create an oval shape. Your two ovals should be about the same size. Pinch off some dough if one is bigger than the other and shape it again. When you have two evenly shaped ovals, gently press both of them to make them a little flat.

Next, we will build the bow. The bow is not just cosmetic, we will be adding an LED light later, so make sure you don't skip this part. To make the bow, take a clump of red play dough and roll it into a sphere. Then roll it into an oval similar to how you made the eyes. Notice that the center of the bow is thinner and has less material. Gently twist the two ends of the oval about 180 degrees. This will help reduce the amount of dough material in the center, but be careful not to break it. Even the bow out and shape it with your fingers. The bow also has two holes in it which give it a nice look. I used the ball-ended tool from the deluxe kit to push into the sides of the play dough at an angle. The back of a pencil with a rounded eraser can also be used to create this effect.

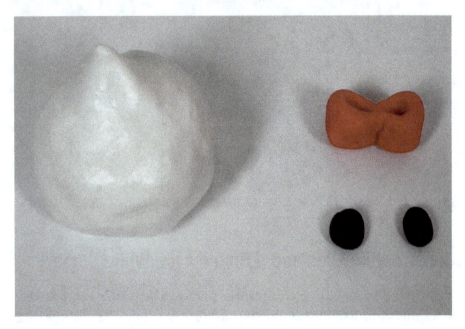

Figure 2-18. *The finished two eyes and bow next to the white slime*

Three Slime Friends

Put the two eyes in front of the slime and place the bow on top of the slime but in front of its point as seen in Figure 2-19. Now you have three happy slimes that are ready for some electrical currents.

Figure 2-19. *The three slimes lined up with the blue slime on the left, the green slime in the middle, and the white slime on the right*

Circuitry for the Buzzer

With our three slimes built, we finally can get started on the circuitry. Think of the blue slime as your character. When you pick up your blue slime and touch the green slime with it, the buzzer will go off and make a loud noise. You can see the wiring in Figure 2-20. For this part, you will need a battery pack and buzzer. The battery pack has a red wire and a black wire. Insert the black wire into the back of the blue slime. After that, insert the red wire into the back or side of the white slime. You will be inserting two wires into the white slime, so leave enough room for a second wire. Also, make sure that you press the red wire pretty deep into the white slime because you want the metal end to make contact with the colored conductive dough on the inside of it.

Take a look at the buzzer. It should look like a circle with a hole on top. The buzzer has a red and black wire as well. Insert the black wire into the back of the green slime. Use the red wire and insert it into the white slime, and make sure you insert it deep enough to make contact with the conductive-colored dough. The white slime will have two red wires, and the blue and green slime will have one black wire each.

When you are finished, turn on the battery pack and pick up the blue slime. See what happens when you touch the green slime and when you touch the white slime. Contact with the green slime should set off the buzzer, while contact with the white slime will not since the white dough is insulating.

Figure 2-20. *The wiring to connect all three slimes with the buzzer*

Bending the LED Light into Shape

The white slime would look cuter if it had an LED light to accompany its bow. We will wire the LED in so that it lights up when the blue slime comes in contact with the bow. We are going to make the white slime's bow light up when it comes into contact with the blue slime. Take a red LED from the red LED bag; the LED lights don't have a color until they are powered on.

Next, we are going to bend the LED into the shape we need. Take note of which of the LED prongs is longer and bend both prongs of the LED light out as far as it will go. Now take the shorter of the two prongs and bend the prong in so it is facing the same direction as the other prong like the example shown in Figure 2-21.

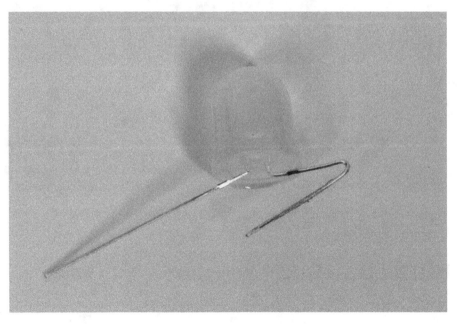

Figure 2-21. *The red LED light is bent into shape. The shorter LED prong is the one with the bend*

After your LED light is bent into shape, you will need to insert it into the white slime. The LED light will go in front of the slime's bow. Temporarily take the slime's bow off and insert the LED light in front of where the bow would go. Insert the straight LED prong into the slime and it should make contact with the colored conductive dough on the inside. The result should look like Figure 2-22.

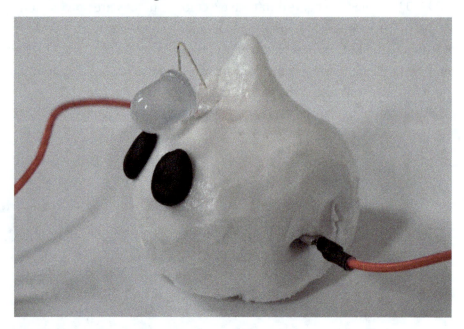

Figure 2-22. *The LED inserted into the white slime with the bow temporarily taken off*

Inserting the LED Light into Place

With the LED in place, take the red bow and put it back on the slime. The bow might end up getting a little cut by the bent LED prong, but that is what we want. The bent LED prong should be in contact with the bow, and the straight LED prong will make contact with the conductive dough inside the slime as shown in Figure 2-23.

Figure 2-23. *The slime with the bow placed behind the LED light*

Testing the LED

Now we need to test if your red LED is working. Push the on switch on the battery pack. Pick up your blue slime and touch it to the white slime's bow. This should make the LED turn on. When you remove the blue slime from the bow, the LED will turn off. You have to make sure that you are touching the white slime's bow and not the white slime itself.

This forms a circuit where electricity goes through the red wire and enters the inside of the white slime where the colored conductive dough is. Then the electricity sees the straight prong of the LED and travels through it toward the LED light and makes it glow. The electricity exits through the bent prong where the bow is touching, and when the blue slime is in contact, it travels through the blue slime, down the black wire in the blue slime, then back to the battery pack. This creates a little circuit that turns on the LED light.

If the LED light doesn't turn on, check the contact points. The LED's straight prong should go down far enough that it touches the colored dough. The bent prong needs good contact with the bow, and it should never touch the colored dough inside the white slime.

Another common mistake is bending the wrong part of the LED prongs. The longer prong is positive, and it should be kept straight. The negative prong, which is shorter, should be bent and touch the bow. If you did this in the wrong order, then you will need to take the LED out and bend the prongs the other way.

Figure 2-24. *The LED light turns on when the blue slime touches the red bow*

Playing with the Slimes

You have now completed all the wiring, and the slimes are ready to play. Grab your blue slime and see how it interacts with the other slimes. When your blue slime touches the green slime, the buzzer will go off. Touch the blue slime to the outer white part of the white slime, and nothing should happen. But when you make contact with the red bow, the LED light will shine brightly as shown in Figure 2-24. The friendly slimes project is now completed. Remember to take some photos of your slime creations!

What's Next?

Now that you have completed these two projects, you may be wondering what you should do next. The best thing to do is to create your own play dough sculptures and make them light up! If you need some inspiration, the official Squishy Circuits website has a lot of projects and tutorials you can try. You don't need to follow these projects exactly, but it may give you some ideas to help you get started.

Paper Circuits

Do your kids love drawing and arts and crafts? Paper circuits allow you to light up your art with glowing LED lights. It combines the best of artistic creativity while teaching your kids how to build simple electrical circuits. There is no complicated wiring involved, because this project uses copper foil tape which tapes flush to paper and can conduct electricity.

- Age range: 5–12

- Difficulty: Beginner

- Amount of time: 1–2 hours

- Learning outcomes: Learn how circuits work; combine circuits with art
- Materials needed:
    - ¼ inch copper foil tape
    - 5mm LED light diodes (3mm and 10mm LEDs also work as long as they accept 3 volts)
    - Penny battery (3 volts)
    - Scotch tape or any nonconductive tape
    - Paper
    - A printer to print the worksheet (you can also borrow a printer at school or work)

Lighting Up a Taiyaki Cat

There are endless possibilities when getting started with paper circuits. To make it simple, I have designed a project template to get started on. For this project, we will be designing a cat with LED lights in its ears which will only light up when we touch the cat's Taiyaki fish snack.

Taiyaki is a Japanese fish-shaped cake made of wheat flour with a red bean filling; no fish were harmed.

First, start by downloading the Taiyaki Cat file from the book's GitHub page and print this page out. The page needs to be printed double-sided with the cat on one side and the wiring guides on the other side. Make sure to print the page in the landscape orientation and set the page flip to be on the short side. When you have your page printed, hold it up to a light and see that the rectangular box on the back side should be around the top of the cat's head as seen in Figure 2-25. It is very important that the page is printed correctly because it affects the placement of the LEDs.

Figure 2-25. *The Taiyaki Cat printed out on printer paper along with the copper tape, two red LEDs, and 3-volt penny battery that we will use later*

Next, fold the paper in half along the dotted line on the back wiring side of the paper. Then bend it back so that the cat is facing the front as seen in Figure 2-26. If this were a book, the page would open from left to right.

Figure 2-26. *The paper folded in half with the cat facing the front*

Wiring the Cat

We are going to start adding the copper tape to the back of the page to create an electrical circuit. The best way to cut the copper tape is by ripping the edges with your fingers. This also makes it easier to peel apart the tape later because it creates an uneven edge.

Place a piece of copper tape along the two places shown next to the battery in Figure 2-27. You can use the copper tape to measure how much you need against the paper before you tear it. I recommend being generous with the copper tape and using a longer piece. Use the copper tape to entirely go through the two battery circles. This is so that when we place the battery down later, the copper tape will make good contact with it. The copper tape should also go a little long on the opposite side so that when we place our second piece of copper tape on it later, it will make good contact.

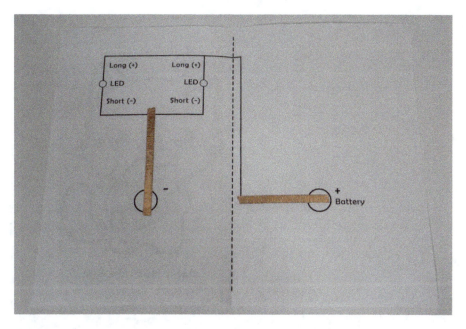

Figure 2-27. *The two pieces of copper tape are placed on the battery circles*

Place the third piece of copper tape on the long line next to the dotted line as seen in Figure 2-28. Place this piece overlapping the copper tape which is already there. It is better to go a little over the existing tape for maximum contact. It is also okay to not follow the line perfectly if your previous piece was a little too short.

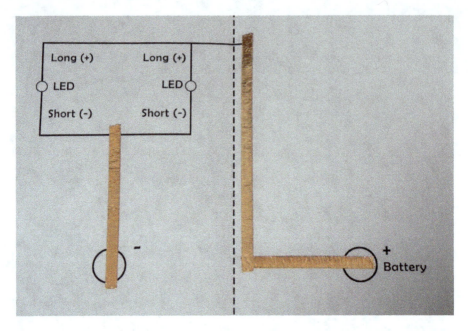

Figure 2-28. *The third piece of copper tape overlapping the already existing copper tape*

For this next step, you will need to place two pieces of copper tape horizontally as shown in Figure 2-29. Have the copper tape overlap any existing copper tape to make good contact with it. The top piece will be a little longer as it has to go through the center fold.

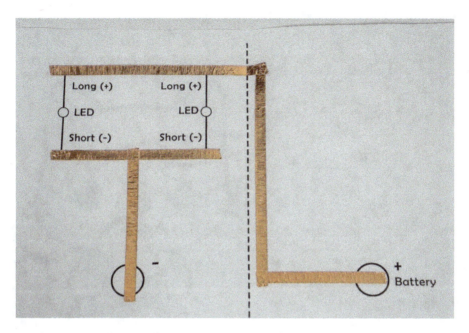

Figure 2-29. *The two horizontal pieces of copper tape placed down*

Lighting Up the Cat

With the main copper tape pieces in place, we are now going to start adding the LED lights to the cat. Flip the page while the page is still open so that you see the side of the cat. Grab the LED light you want to use and poke through the paper in the center of the cat's ear like in Figure 2-30. Then pull the LED light through so the bottom is flush against the paper and it is standing straight.

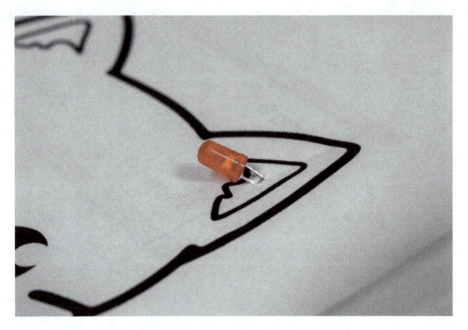

Figure 2-30. *The LED light is used to poke a hole through the cat's ear*

We are now going to bend the LED into place. Start by flipping the page over so that you see the LED's two prongs. One of the prongs is longer than the other; take note of which one. Bend both prongs out so that they create a straight line like in Figure 2-31. The paper will tear easily, so I recommend holding the plastic part of the LED on the other side while you are bending the prongs.

After your prongs are bent, put the longer prong adjacent to the side of the page that says "Long," and the shorter side will go on the bottom next to "Short."

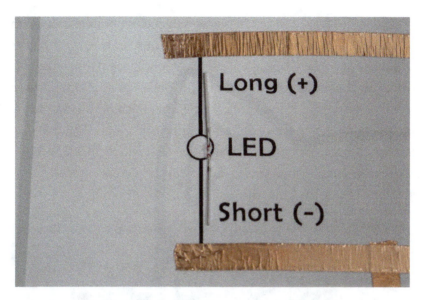

Figure 2-31. *The LED bent into shape with the longer prong on top next to Long and the shorter prong on the bottom next to Short*

Repeat the previous two steps and put the second LED into the other cat's ear. You can see the two LEDs in place in Figure 2-32.

Figure 2-32. *The two LEDs are placed in the cat's ears*

Now that the two LEDs are in place, we need to connect them with the rest of the circuit. You will need four pieces of copper tape for this step. Place a piece of copper tape along each wire and have it touch the copper tape above or below as seen in Figure 2-33. Make sure the two pieces of copper tape on the LED don't touch each other because this would create a short circuit and stop the LED from lighting up. It is also good to use your fingers to press the copper tape around the LED wire firmly. This is usually the weakest point of contact in the electrical circuit, so you really want the copper tape to hug the LED wire.

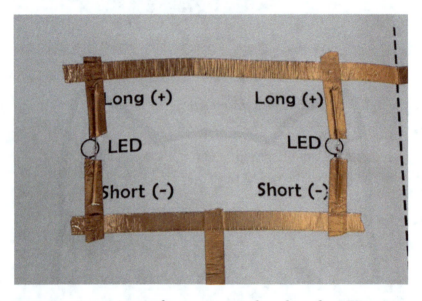

Figure 2-33. *Four pieces of copper tape placed on the LED wires*

Now our circuit is almost complete, but it lacks a power source. On the right side of the page with the battery circle labeled with a + which is a positive current, we are going to place our 3-volt penny battery here. Check the battery and one side will be labeled with a +. Have the side with the + sign facing down. Test that your battery is facing the right direction by closing the paper and pressing down on the fish.

If the LED lights up, you are good to secure your battery down with regular nonconductive scotch tape as seen in Figure 2-34. Place one piece of tape on the top and one piece on the bottom. Leave enough exposed area on the battery so that it can make contact with the copper tape on top when you close the page. Closing the page is what completes the circuit!

Figure 2-34. *The battery with the + side facing down and secured with scotch tape. Make sure you don't cover the entire battery*

Close the page and press down on the battery, which happens to be under the fish. Watch the two LED lights in the cat's ears glow when you press the fish! You can see the LEDs light up in Figure 2-35. Congratulations, you have finished the project and made a parallel circuit with LED lights. I highly recommend going back and coloring the cat to make it unique and your own kids' artwork. You can even put your art on the fridge when you're done!

Figure 2-35. *The finished project where pressing down on the battery behind the fish makes the two LEDs light up*

Troubleshooting

If none of your LED lights have lit up or only one of them lights up, there are a few common mistakes we can address. The most important part of creating a paper circuit is creating a good connection. Check that all the copper tape segments are overlapping each other completely. The overlap should create a square that bumps out a little, and the copper tape may extend out a little further with excess. It is also good to apply some pressure at the points where the copper tape intersects each other to secure the connection.

You can also go back and check your LED lights. The LEDs have a short prong and a long prong. It is very important that the long prong goes on top next to Long, and the short prong goes on the bottom.

It is also good to check that the two pieces of copper tape on the LED lights aren't touching each other (which would create a short circuit). The weakest connection of the circuit is usually the contact between the copper tape and the LED light's prongs. Make sure that the LED prongs are in the center of the copper tape and press very firmly to reinforce the connection. You can even use your nails to firmly press the tape into the LED's prong.

Another place to check is the copper tape around the battery. It should be long enough and positioned so that when you close the page, the copper tape on top clamps down and touches the top of the battery. The battery is also very directional and will only work with the + side facing down on the + side of the page. By looking at these few common mistakes, you should be able to have a working paper circuit!

What's Next?

Now that you have completed your Taiyaki Cat paper circuit, it is a good opportunity to create your very own paper circuits. You can experiment on a piece of paper and build your own simple circuits. Once you have a good idea of how to make an LED light up, then you can draw your own original drawings and add paper circuits to the back of it. These circuits can even be used with holiday cards, Halloween costumes, cardboard, and more! The possibilities are endless.

Conclusion

It is never too early to get your kids started with technology. Learning about circuits is one of the best ways to get started as it is very entertaining and intuitive. Squishy circuits are great for young kids because they can learn about circuits by lighting up their play dough creations. Paper circuits is another fun project for kids who love arts and crafts; it lets them light up their creations. In the next chapter, we will look at block coding projects which is a good way to teach kids about coding in an easy and entertaining way.

CHAPTER 3

Getting Started with Block Coding

Block programming is the best way for kids and first-time coders to learn how to program. It is great for kids ages 8 and all the way up to 16. Block coding is good for young kids because it is a drag-and-drop style and does not require much typing. However, it is just as useful for kids of any age because it teaches simple code concepts like "if" statements, "while" loops, or even how variables work. Block coding also encourages creativity because it is easy to pick up; kids will explore and show you what they can create!

Do your kids love robots? If they don't, they definitely will after they learn how to program one! In this chapter, we will learn how to block code with two types of robots. We will build and program a Lego-style robotic crab using the Makerzoid set. This set is great because it is a more economical version of the Lego Spike but with all the same bricks and even more instructions and projects. We will also be programming the mBot which is closer to a more traditional robot with wheels and a line-following sensor. What sets the mBot apart from other robots is that all the tedious steps like GPIO pin wiring are done for you already. This lets your kids go straight to the fun part, which is assembling the robot together and then getting straight into the coding which lets the robot move!

© Cassandra Chin 2025
C. Chin, *Raising Young Coders*, https://doi.org/10.1007/979-8-8688-1393-1_3

Lego Crab

In this project, kids will learn how to build and program their own robotic crab. Your kids will have a lot of fun building the crab with Lego pieces, and since they are just bricks, they can add their own creative touch to their robotic crab. Your kids will also learn about different types of sensors. The crab has one motor for movement and one distance sensor for detecting when something is near it. The coding for the crab is all done in a Scratch ecosystem with block coding. There are an infinite number of possibilities for how you want to program the crab with your kids. You can make it dance left and right, play sounds, and make it look silly!

You may have heard of the Lego Spike before which is Lego's STEM education system. The problem is it is very expensive, priced at almost $500 a kit, which means only some school districts and camps can afford it. We will be using the Makerzoid which is similar to the Lego Spike but priced much more affordably at only about $100. My kid sister who is 12 years old has used the Lego Spike in school before, but she tried the Makerzoid at home and she didn't find it that much harder to build with.

- Age range: 8–14

- Difficulty: Beginner to intermediate

- Amount of time: 1–2 afternoons

- Learning outcomes: Learn block coding, building with Legos, how motors and sensors work

- Materials needed: Makerzoid Robot Master (standard or premium both work), two AA batteries

Build Instructions

Both the Makerzoid Robot Master Standard set and the Makerzoid Robot Master Premium set will work for the crab project. When deciding which set you want to get, the main difference is that the standard set comes with one motor and one sensor, while the premium set comes with two motors and two sensors along with extra building parts. The Makerzoid app helps you by letting you select which set you own, and they will only show you the projects you have parts for. The premium set is better if you want to try other projects in the app that require more motors and sensors; otherwise, the standard set will work just as well for this project.

When you open your Makerzoid, you will find an instruction manual in the box. It only has beginner projects that don't involve programming, so I don't recommend using it. You may also find a card that says "Course Instructions" on the back. If you redeem the card in the app, it will give you access to their video guides. However, you can build all the sets and do all the programming without the videos, and you won't need them for this project.

The first thing you should do is install the Makerzoid app on a tablet or phone. This is where all your Lego instructions will be. When you are selecting a kit, make sure you select the kit you own. The sets and instructions available to you will change based on which kit you select. To find the instructions for the crab we are building, scroll down on the left bar to "Jr. Programming" and find "Crab (AI)." Then click the "Build" button to download the instructions, and you can start building.

How much help your kids will need to build the crab will depend on their age. For younger kids, you should sit together with them and help them find pieces and build the set with them. For kids who are more familiar with Legos, you can step away so that they have the opportunity to problem-solve. But you should still be ready to jump in and help if they get stuck on a step or just really can't find that piece. You can see what the completed crab looks like in Figure 3-1.

Figure 3-1. *This is what the crab looks like when completed. The distance sensor is located in front of the crab on the bottom, while the motor which powers the legs is located in the back*

Notes:

Remember to put batteries into your power brick. Slide the top white cover off and insert two double AA batteries. Close the cover and press the power button on the short slide. If you see a light, then you are good to go!

The technic axles in the online instructions don't have guides for measuring. Instead, you should measure the axle against a piece that is the same number of bricks. If you need a technic axle that is 8 long, it should be the same length as a technic brick which is 8 long (8 dots on top).

The crab also has a tricky gear part you have to insert from the bottom. While you insert this, you also have to keep the white pieces aligned. To help with alignment, you can insert two temporary technic axles through while you put the gears in place.

Programming Instructions

After you finish building the crab, you will need to program it with your kids. There are three buttons on the app: "Build," "Code," and "Control." I recommend ignoring the "Control" button because that lets you directly control the crab which takes away from the coding experience. You want your kids to be playing with code blocks, not controlling the crab with a virtual joystick!

Click the "Code" button, and there will be two pop-ups, "Official" and "Create." You will want to click "Create" which gives you a blank Scratch block coding interface. Do not use the "Official" button for your code, because you cannot save your work in this mode. Coding the crab isn't that hard, and we will have step-by-step instructions in this book.

Making the Crab Move

The programming is done in a block coding Scratch interface which makes it very easy for kids to learn coding. Block coding is one of the best ways for kids to have fun creating programs without having to learn coding syntax. You can see what the block coding interface looks like in Figure 3-2. The very left panel is a navigation bar that helps sort all the coding blocks by different categories. The coding blocks are in the secondmost left panel. You use them by scrolling through them, and you can drag and drop them on the left, which is the script area. The script area is where all your executable code goes. It is okay to have unused blocks in the script area. The code only gets executed if it is connected to the green flag or another block that is connected to it.

Right now, the crab just looks cute, but we want it to move. The crab's main body and most of its weight comes from the power brick. It also has a motor on its back. The power brick supplies power to the motor, and that single motor will power all the gears and move the legs of the crab.

To make the crab move, drag the first box called "motor [port1] direction [clockwise] speed(0-12) (6)" into the script area. Click the green flag to make the crab move, and to pause it, click the yellow pause button. You can see an example of this in Figure 3-2.

When you press the green flag, you may get asked to pair the power brick with your device. To do this, turn the power brick on with the power button and put it near your device. Then you can get started!

Don't touch the crab or the buttons on the power brick while the crab is in motion. It is very easy to get your fingers pinched! Stop the crab using the pause button on the app.

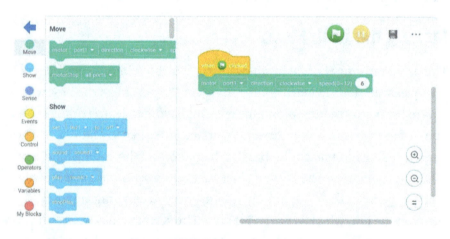

Figure 3-2. *Block code to make the crab move*

Initially, the crab always walks toward its left at the same speed. Try experimenting with the [clockwise] drop-down as seen in Figure 3-3. This will reverse the direction of the motor to spin the other way. Press the green flag and watch it walk toward its right instead.

You can change the speed the crab walks by modifying the speed value. This will make the motor on the back spin faster or slower. Only numbers between (0–12) will work. Does changing the crab's speed to 10 increase or decrease its speed?

We are only using one motor so keep the motor on [port1].

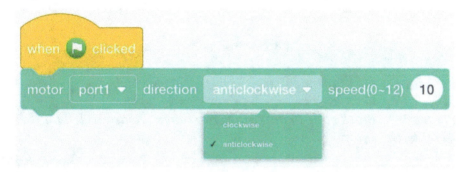

Figure 3-3. *Block code to make the crab move toward its right*

Making the Crab Dance

The crab can now move to its left or right, but it would be cooler if it could dance. The first step to teaching the crab how to dance is teaching it how to walk to the side and stop.

We are going to teach the crab how to walk to its left for three seconds, then stop as seen in Figure 3-4. Find the "wait" block under Controls and put it under the motor block. Set the wait time to three seconds. Then find the "motorStop" block under "Move" and put it under the wait block. Click the green flag and watch the crab stop all on its own.

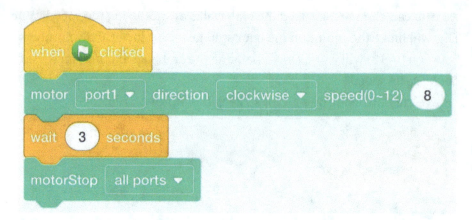

Figure 3-4. *Block code to make the crab move toward its left for three seconds, then stop*

We are going to make the crab dance by making it walk to its left for three seconds, and then to its right for three seconds. The code blocks for this can be seen in Figure 3-5. First, temporarily drag the "motorStop" block out of the way. Find another motor and wait block and put it under the existing two. Set the speed and wait time to be identical to your other two motor and wait blocks. Change the second motor block to be [anticlockwise] so that the crab will walk in the other direction. Last, put the "motorStop" block back in its place at the end. Press the green flag and watch the crab dance! This is a good time to save your work using the save button in the top-right corner.

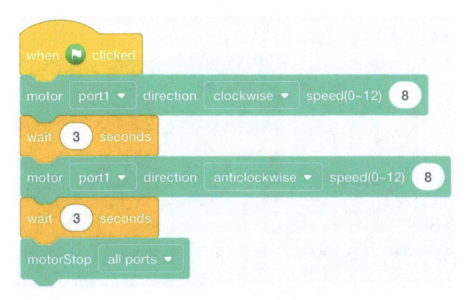

Figure 3-5. *Block code to make the crab dance by moving to its left for three seconds, then to its right for three seconds*

Activating the Crab with a Distance Sensor

We are going to make the crab dance on its own when you wave your hand near the infrared distance sensor. The sensor is located under the crab and facing forward. Infrared distance sensors have two sensor holes. The sending sensor will emit a light, and that light will find the nearest object in front, and then bounce back at the receiving sensor. When you move your hand closer to the sensor, the light comes back with a stronger signal, so the distance sensor knows you are close.

To program the distance sensor, we are going to first find all the blocks we will need to program it. In the Sense category, look for "distanceSensor (0~6) [sensor1]" and drag it to the scripting area. Next, go to the Operators category and find "blank < 50." Drag it to the scripting area and change value 50 to a 3. Go to the Control category and drag an "if then" and a "forever" box which should both look like clamshells. All the blocks can be seen as laid out in Figure 3-6. We will combine them in the next step.

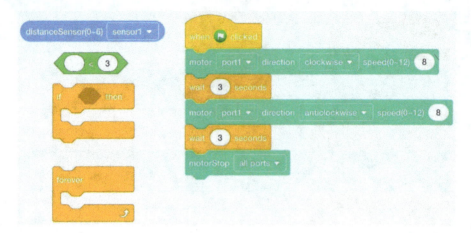

Figure 3-6. *The code blocks needed for the distance sensor laid out*

The next step is to combine all the blocks as seen in Figure 3-7. Drag the "distanceSensor" block into the blank space of the "blank < 3" block on the left. They should merge into one long block. Next, drag this long block into the diamond space in the "if then" block. It should make the "if then" block look like a very long clamshell. Next, take your large "if then" block and insert it inside the "forever" block.

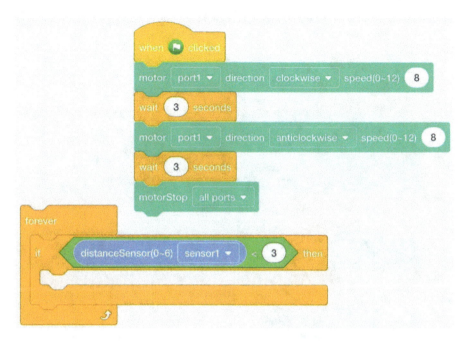

Figure 3-7. *The code blocks partially combined for the distance sensor*

We still need to merge the left and right code blocks. Currently, all the code blocks we created aren't connected to the green flag, so it won't change anything. Drag the first motor block and detach it from the green flag. You will end up with a clump of blocks. Move this clump of blocks you just detached and put it inside the "if then" block clamshell. All the blocks will be combined. Drag the forever block under the green flag. You can see what it looks like when all the blocks are combined in Figure 3-8.

73

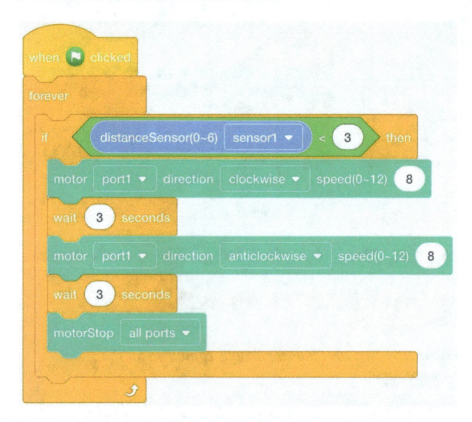

Figure 3-8. *The finished code blocks for the infrared distance sensor*

Press the green flag to run the program. All the code blocks will stay highlighted yellow because they are always running in a forever loop. The distance sensor is always actively checking if something is nearby. Wave your hand in front of the crab's distance sensor to watch it dance! After it is done dancing, you can wave your hand in front of it to make it dance again. If you want to deactivate the sensor and stop the crab, press the yellow pause button. Remember to save your work in the top-right corner.

Playing Music and More

The basic functionalities of the crab are done, but it is always fun to see
what else we can make the crab do. The fun part of programming is getting
creative and making our robotic crab look extra silly.

I will show you an example of how you can add music to the crab while
it dances. Find the "Show" category and grab the "play [music1]" block. Put
this block directly above the first "motor" block. We also want to make the
crab stop playing the music when it is done dancing. Find the "stopPlay"
block and put it under the "motorStop" block. All the code blocks can be
found in Figure 3-9. The sound will come out of your mobile device, so
make sure you don't have it on mute and turn up the volume. When you
are ready, press the green flag and wave your hand in front of the crab's
distance sensor to activate it.

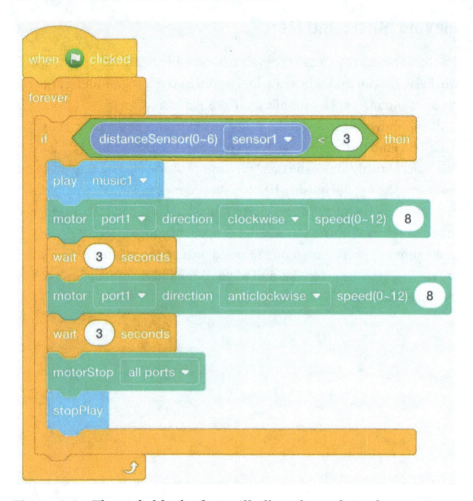

Figure 3-9. *The code blocks that will allow the crab to play music while it dances*

In the next part, I will show you how to make the crab dance for longer before it stops. Find the "repeat" block from the Control category. Set the number of repeats to three. Drag the first "motor" block out which will come with a lot of blocks and put it on the side. If you added music to your crab, drag the "stopPlay" block off and put it back in under the "play [music1]" block. Put the "motor" block cluster inside your new "repeat

3" block. Take your repeat block cluster and drag it in between the "play [music1]" block and the "stopPlay" block. You can see an example of this in Figure 3-10.

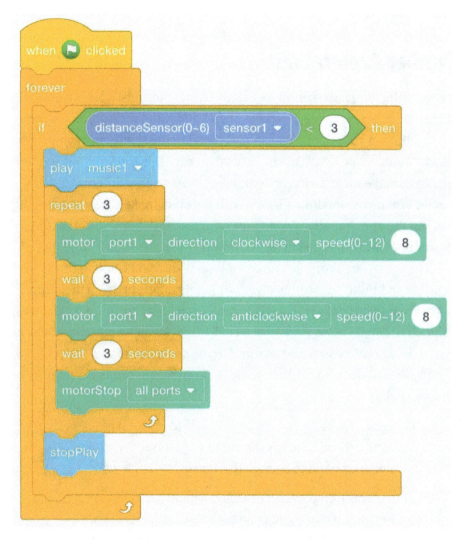

Figure 3-10. *The code blocks for the crab with the repeat 3 loop*

When you are ready, run your program with the play button and watch your crab dance from side to side. If you want your crab to dance for a longer or shorter time, change the number in the repeat block. Remember to save your work!

Further Exploration

At this point, you have completed all the coding exercises for the crab. The Scratch block coding interface has a lot of room for experimenting and coding on your own. You can try changing the numbers in your code blocks to see what it does to your crab. You can also add your own code blocks to make the crab move in different ways or play different music tracks. When you are done playing with the crab, make sure you save your work in the app. It is also a good idea to press the power button on the power brick so you don't run out of power.

The great part about the Makerzoid set is that you can tear down your projects and build something else completely different using their app instructions. There are hundreds of projects in their app, and it can be difficult to decide which one to try. I will offer you some recommendations based on whether you have the standard or premium set.

If you own the standard set, there are some great projects under Jr. Programming:

- Crocodile: This is a fun project because it moves forward and chomps the crocodile's mouth when you put your hand in front of the sensor.

- Color Sorting Machine: This is a good project to try because it will let you use the sensor to detect color instead of distance. It is easy to build, so you can get started on programming more quickly.

If you own the premium set, try some of the Advanced Programming projects:

- Woodpecker: If your child likes the crab project, another interesting one is to build a Woodpecker that will dance around when you wave your hand in front of it.

- Dual Motor Lunar Rover: This is a simple project that gives you a lot of flexibility since one motor steers the front wheel while the other motor powers the back wheel. This is similar to how a real car operates, so creating a program to drive it can be a lot of fun.

mBot Line Follower

For this project, we will be teaching a robot how to follow a heart-shaped line. It will also detect color and speed up and slow down based on what it sees. Robots are a lot of fun for kids of all ages and backgrounds. It is interesting to watch robots move, but it is a different experience when you are the one who programmed it to move. A traditional robot powered by an Arduino requires learning about GPIO pins and hardware gimmicks, but the mBot simplifies this and lets you get straight into the coding.

For this project, we will be using the latest version of the mBot called the mBot2. The mBot2 itself has a lot of potential for different projects. It supports both block coding and Python, but we will be using block coding for our line follower project. The mBot2 also comes with a variety of sensors, including the quad RGB sensor, distance sensor, microphone and speaker, and the programmable CyberPi. This gives you a lot of options for how you want to program your mBot2 and what you want it to do.

- Age range: 8–16

- Difficulty: Intermediate

- Amount of time: 1–2 afternoons

- Learning outcomes: Learn block coding, building with screws, and how to use a line follower sensor

- Materials needed:

    - mBot2 (the original mBot has different hardware and won't work for these instructions)

    - A desktop or laptop computer to program the mBot (an inexpensive Chromebook will also work)

    - White poster paper, black, green, and yellow masking tape for the track

---

Tip   A phone or tablet with the official mBlock app will also work with the program in this chapter. However, I recommend spending the time to set up a computer to connect to the mBot. This will give a better experience and allow for more advanced projects where you use a keyboard to program.

Building the mBot2

The first step is building the mBot2. The mBot2 box comes with lots of instructions and parts. Find the Quick Start Guide mini book which has all the assembly instructions for your mBot2.

The instruction booklet comes with a step-by-step guide on how to assemble the robot, but I found it a little confusing to follow. Building the robot is very simple, but the pictures in the instructions are very small and some steps can be difficult to follow. To make it less frustrating for your kids, I recommend assembling the mBot with them and following a few tips:

- The assembly instructions for the robot start in the middle of the booklet. Ignore the first few pages and start on step 1. This will save you some time and confusion since all the sensors are already assembled and there is nothing to do until step 1.

- To make searching for the right-sized screw easier, there is a 1:1 scale blue box for each step. Place your screw on the screw diagram to see if it's the right size.

- The wiring can get very confusing because the diagrams are small, and the blue metal casing has a lot of holes. It is important that you spend the time to get the wires in the right holes so that they are out of the way and won't get caught on anything.

- If you want your wires to look neat and tidy, you can fit them in the space between the blue metal casing and the mBot2 Shield while you're screwing them together. Doing this is a little tricky, but completely optional. If you can't get the wires to fit, it is better to leave them hanging than to damage them.

Connecting the Robot

Once you have the robot built, visit the mBlock website (`https://mblock.makeblock.com/`) and that is where we will code the robot to make it move. They have both a Block-based coding editor and a Python coding editor. For our exercise, we will be using the Block-based editor.

The next step is to connect your mBot to your computer. We are going to use the mLink software to connect. If you see text that says "Switch to mLink," click that to make sure you are using mLink (and if there is no text or it says "Switch to direct connection," you are fine). Click the "Connect" button as seen in Figure 3-11, and it will open a pop-up saying you need mLink. Wait a few more seconds while it is still open, and it will show you a download button to download mLink. You can also download mLink for Windows, Mac, Linux, or Chromebook from this website:

`https://mblock.makeblock.com/en/download/mlink/.`

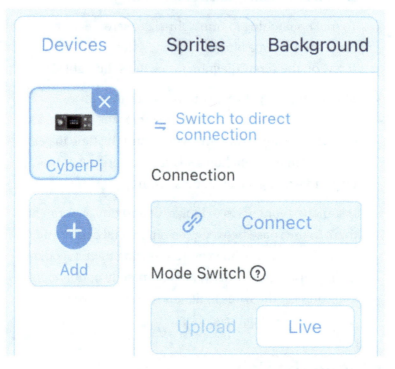

Figure 3-11. *The connect button is in the center of the cluster of menu items*

You will need your mBot2 plugged in to the computer and powered on to install mLink. Directly connect the mBot to your computer and turn on the power button on the front. Now run the mLink installer and install the device driver on the last step. Once you have mLink installed and running, press the same "Connect" button, and you will get a different pop-up as shown in Figure 3-12. Then press the second "Connect" button in the pop-up to control your mBot from your computer.

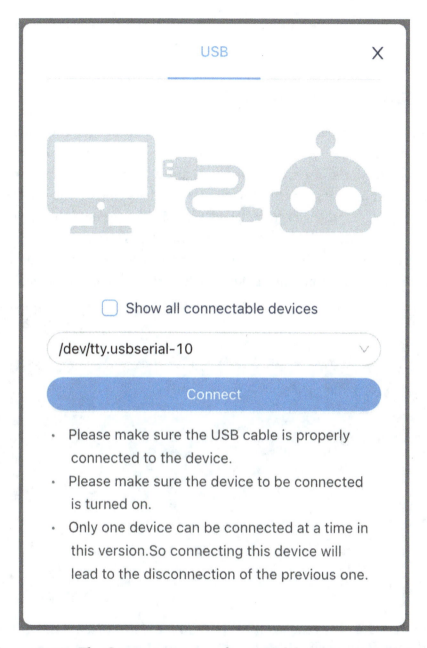

USB   X

Show all connectable devices

/dev/tty.usbserial-10

Connect

· Please make sure the USB cable is properly
  connected to the device.
· Please make sure the device to be connected
  is turned on.
· Only one device can be connected at a time in
  this version.So connecting this device will
  lead to the disconnection of the previous one.

Figure 3-12. *The Connect pop-up after mLink has been installed,*
and the mBot is plugged in via USB. The text in the drop-down will
likely be different on your computer

I recommend creating an account with Makeblock so that you can save your work with the save button. Always remember to save your work!

Creating a Heart-Shaped Track

Before we can program the mBot to follow a line, we are going to build a line for it to follow. To make it more fun, we are going to build the robot a track in the shape of a heart as seen in Figure 3-13. The line follower robot works best when it sees a black line on a white background. We will use poster paper for the background, and it should be large enough that we can build a track on it for the robot. Use your black masking tape to draw a heart on the page. I found it easier to use a pencil to sketch where the ends of the tape should touch as a guide for where to place the tape down.

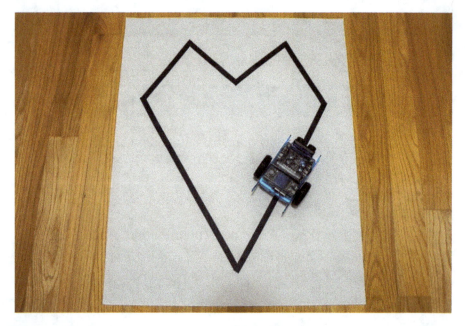

Figure 3-13. *The finished track built in the shape of a heart, with the mBot on it for scale*

With the track finished, now we need to program the robot to follow the line.

Following a Line

The mBot2 is very good at following lines and can follow a track. It has four sensors at the front which can see color. Depending on which sensor sees the color of the line or the color of the background, the robot can be programmed to know when it goes off track and center itself.

Before we get to coding the robot, we need to define some variables. In the block coding editor, find the "Variables" tab which is orange. We will need to create four variables, and each variable will affect the robot in different ways:

- base_power: Speed of the robot

- kp: Turn speed of the robot

- left_power: Actual speed of the left wheel

- right_power: Actual speed of the right wheel

Click the "Make a Variable" button as seen in Figure 3-14 and create your four variables.

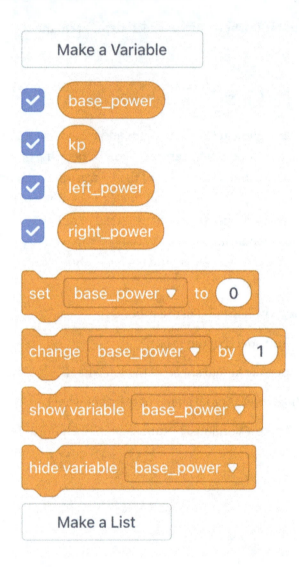

Figure 3-14. *Creating four variables for the line follower robot*

With our variables created, we can now start programming the robot. Look under the yellow "Events" tab and find the "when button [] pressed" block. Click the drop-down and set it to B. The mBot has a controller attached to the back called the CyberPi which has an A button and a B button. With the "when button B pressed" block, we are programming the mBot to do something when we press the B button.

Next, we have to define our variables inside the program. Even though we defined the variables earlier, they won't help us unless we use them. Go back to the orange "Variables" tab and find the "set [] to ()" block. Drag two of these blocks down under the previous block. Then set the first one to "set [base_power] to (20)" and the second block to "set [kp] to (0.5)." You can see an example of the finished outcome in Figure 3-15. With these two variables, we are defining the speed of the robot and the turn adjustment value for line following.

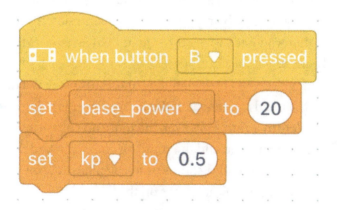

Figure 3-15. *Creating a button-pressed event and defining variables*

When designing a line follower robot, the left and right wheels must turn at different speeds so that it can adjust itself to stay on the line. On a right turn, the left wheel will speed up to make the turn. On a left turn, the right wheel will speed up. Even on a straight line, the robot will need to turn left and right to recenter itself on its path. We created the "left_power" and the "right_power" variables so that we can independently control the speed of each wheel.

For this part, we will need to get the extensions to control the mBot's sensors. Make sure you have the "Devices" tab selected on the bottom-left panel. Then, click the blue button with a plus sign located under the block category labels to open the "Extension Center." Add the "*mBot2shield*" and the "*Quad RBG Sensor*" extensions. If you don't see these extensions, you may be looking at "Sprite Extensions." If this happens, go back and make sure the "Devices" tab is selected.

Now, we are going to build the code for controlling the "left_power" variable, which is how fast the left wheel should go. You can see the blocks combined in Figure 3-16. Drag the multiplication box under Operators. Then find kp under Variables and put it in the first slot of the multiplication box. Then find the "quad rgb sensor (1) deviation (-100~100)" box under the "Quad RGB Sensor" tab and put it in the second slot. If you don't see this box, then you need to get the "Quad RGB Sensor" extension as mentioned earlier.

The "quad rgb sensor (1) deviation (-100~100)" block is a direct reading from the quad rgb sensor. If the line follower is going perfectly on the line, it will return a zero. However, the more off course toward the right it is, the higher the number, and the more off course toward the left, the lower the number. This reading helps us to calculate how much the robot should turn left or right so that it stays on the line.

Figure 3-16. *The blocks for kp * quad rgb sensor (1) deviation (-100~100)*

For this next step, find the addition block under the "Operators" category. Drag "base_power" from the "Variables" tab into the first slot of the "addition" block. Then take your block from the last step and put it into the second slot. You can see the result in Figure 3-17.

base_power
+
kp
*
quad rgb sensor
1
deviation (-100~100)

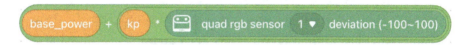

Figure 3-17. *The base_power variable is in the first slot of the addition block, and the previous block cluster is in the second slot*

Now find the "multiplication" block in the "Operators" tab. Set the first slot to –1. Then drag your block cluster from the previous step into the second slot as seen in Figure 3-18.

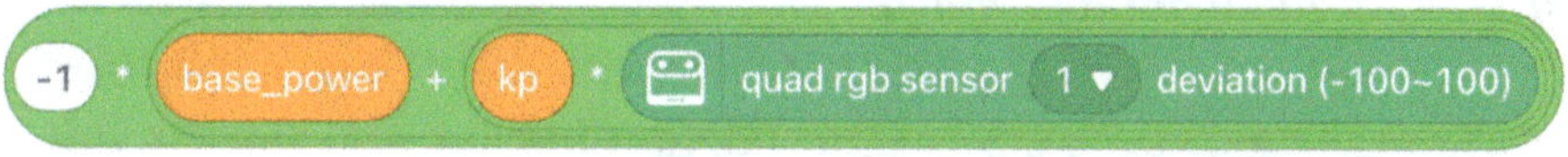
-1
*
base_power
+
kp
*
quad rgb sensor
1
deviation (-100~100)

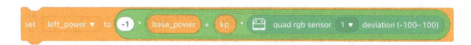

Figure 3-18. *The multiplication block with –1 in slot 1 and the block cluster in slot 2*

We are almost done with the code for controlling the left wheel. Drag over the set block from the "Variables" tab. Click the drop-down and put it on "left_power." Then take the previous block cluster we made and put it where the 0 currently is as seen in Figure 3-19.

set
left_power
to
-1
*
base_power
+
kp
*
quad rgb sensor
1
deviation (-100~100)

Figure 3-19. *The left_power block completed*

With the "left_power" block completed, we now need to build the "right_power" block which will control the speed of the right wheel. The first block part, "kp * quad rgb sensor," is the same as the "left_power block." You can copy this block section by right-clicking the block from the previous steps and duplicating it.

Drag a "subtraction" block from the "Operators" tab. Then find the "base_power" block from the "Variables" tab and put that in the first slot of the "subtraction" block. Now put the block cluster that you duplicated earlier into the second slot as seen in Figure 3-20.

Figure 3-20. *The subtraction block encases the base_power block and the duplicated block cluster*

The "right_power" block is almost done. Find the "set" block under the "Variables" tab and use the drop-down menu to set it to "right_power." Then put the block cluster you just created where the 0 is as seen in Figure 3-21.

Figure 3-21. *The completed right_power block*

We have assigned values to both the "left_power" and "right_power" variables, but now we need to use these variables to make the robot move. Under the "mBot2 Chassis" tab, find the block seen in Figure 3-22. Then go to the "Variables" tab and use the "right_power" block in the first slot and the "left_power" block in the second slot.

Figure 3-22. *The motor block that rotates the left and right wheel independently*

Now that we have all the blocks we need, we need to combine them and add them to our "when button B pressed" block so that the code blocks will execute. Go to the "Control" tab and drag over a "forever" block. Put the three blocks you created into the "forever" block in the same order you created them. Then attach the "forever" block under the "set kp" block as shown in Figure 3-23.

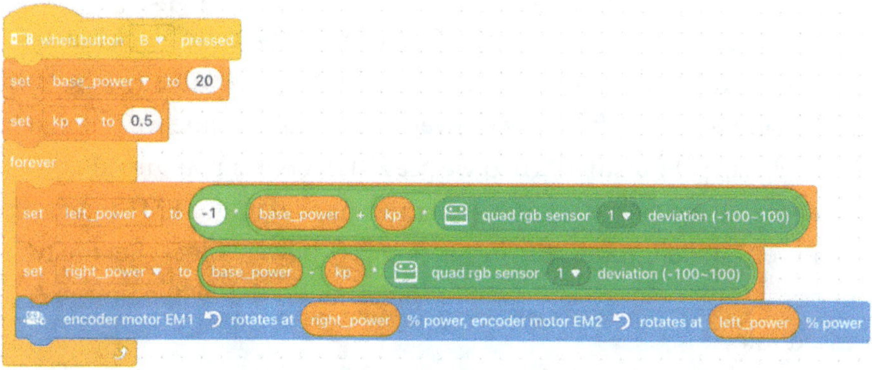

Figure 3-23. *All the blocks we created are now connected to the "when button B pressed" block which will allow the code to execute*

Now that the coding is finished, we need to upload our code to the mBot and test it. The mBot has Bluetooth support to upload wirelessly with a special Bluetooth adapter from MakeBlock, but I find the direct connection with a cable much easier and more reliable to use. Use a cable to connect the mBot to your computer and connect it using the connect button. Make sure you are on "Upload" mode and not "Live" mode. Now click "Upload Code" and send your code to the mBot. When it has finished uploading, unplug the cable from the mBot and test it on the heart track you have built.

To test the robot, first put your track on the floor. I have tried putting the track on the table before, and it usually ends with the mBot dropping onto the floor. Set your robot on the track and press the B triangle button to let it run. To stop the robot, currently, the only way is to flip off the power switch, but we will fix this in the next section.

Teaching the Robot How to Stop

You should have encountered a few issues with the robot. The mBot is incredibly slow as it goes around the track, and there is no way to stop it. First, we are going to teach the robot how to stop using the A button so that we don't have to power cycle it every time we want it to stop.

To stop the robot, we are going to implement the code blocks seen in Figure 3-23. To start programming on the A button, we will need the "when button A pressed" block from the "Events" tab. All the code we put under this block will get executed when we press the A button on the mBot.

To stop all motor movement, find the "encoder motor EM1 rotates at () % power, encoder motor EM2 rotates at () % power" block. Set the two numerical values to zero and drag the block under the "when button A pressed" block.

To get the robot to stop what it's doing, we need to stop other code blocks from executing. Find the "stop" block under the Control tab and connect it to the "when button A pressed" block cluster. Use the drop-down menu to change the stop to stop "other scripts in sprite." You can see the code blocks put together for button A in Figure 3-24.

Figure 3-24. *This code block will execute when button A is pressed, and it will stop the robot from moving or executing scripts*

With your code for button A finished, you now need to upload it to your robot. Plug the cable to connect your mBot to your computer and press the connect button again to connect the mBot as a device. Then upload your code. When it has finished uploading, unplug your robot and put it down on the track to test the start and stop buttons.

Using Color Detection to Speed Up and Slow Down

The mBot is very good at following the line, and we can even start and stop the robot with the A and B buttons. However, the mBot moves at a very slow pace, and it would be more fun if it could go faster. Currently, we can change the speed of the robot by raising the base_power value. The problem with raising the speed is that it will make the robot worse at following the line, and it may go off track around corners.

To stop the robot from going off track by going too fast, we are going to put colored tape on the track to tell the robot when it should go fast and when it should slow down before going around a turn. Like a traffic light, we are going to use green tape to go fast and yellow tape to slow down. You can see the tape placement in Figure 3-25. The green tape goes on the inside sections and the yellow tape is on the outside right before the turns. Use two pieces of tape side by side to make it a little thicker. This will increase the chance that the mBot sees the tape.

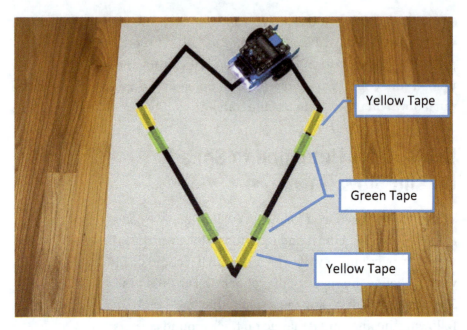

Figure 3-25. *The tape is placed on the long sides of the heart. The green tape goes on the inside edges, while the yellow tape goes on the outside edges right before the turns*

We placed the colored tape down, but the robot won't do anything unless we program it. First, we want the robot to use its quad RGB sensor to look for colors. Then when it picks up the color green, it will speed up, and if it sees the color yellow, it should slow down.

We are first going to program the mBot to speed up when it sees green. Drag over an "if" block from the "Control" tab. Then go to the "Operators" tab and find an "or" block. Next, scroll down to the Quad RGB Sensor tab which is an extension we added earlier. Find the "quad rgb sensor () probe () detects () ?" block and drag two of them over and put them inside the "or" block. Change the first quad rgb block to "(3) L1 detects green" Change the first block to "(2) R1 detects green." The mBot has four color sensors, and this lets us use the two sensors closest to the middle. You can see the combined blocks in Figure 3-26.

Figure 3-26. *The blocks for using the RGB sensor to do something if it sees the color green*

Now the mBot has a way to see green, and we need to program it to do something when it sees the green tape. Inside the if statement, drag a "set base_power" block from the "Variables" tab and set it to 40. This higher number will tell it to speed up. Then go to the LED tab and find the "display" block with five color blocks following. Change the five colored blocks to green blocks. When the mBot sees green, this will give us an easy indicator that it saw green. Put both blocks inside the "if" statement. Then drag your "if" block inside the "forever" block from the main program. You can see the "if" block cluster combined and attached the main program in Figure 3-27. Feel free to test your program and watch your robot speed up when it sees the green tape.

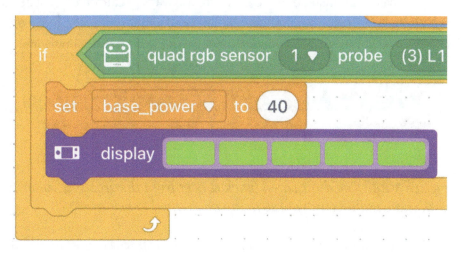

Figure 3-27. *The "if" block cluster attached to the main program lowers the base_power and changes the display color to green*

Now we need to program the robot to slow down when it goes around a corner. We already have the yellow tape around the corners, we just need to program it. The code for speeding up and slowing down is similar, so we can borrow some of the code from the last segment. Duplicate the entire "if" block we built for detecting green and place it under the previous "if" block, but also inside the "forever" block.

We will need to change some of the values in the blocks. For the first part, change both blocks that say "detects green" to "detects yellow." Then change the value of "base_power" to 15 which will slow down the robot. Last, change the "display" block and set all the colored blocks to yellow. You can see all the changes in Figure 3-28. Upload your code and watch your robot go! This change should help your mBot stay on track and not slip off course.

If your mBot doesn't see the colored tape, your code blocks might be off, or it could be the color calibration of the quad RGB sensor. I had an issue where I had a darker green roll of tape, and when the mBot rolled over it, it saw cyan instead of green. There are ways to calibrate the sensor, but the easiest fix is to set the "detects" block to a different color and see what works. For example, if you are having trouble with the yellow tape, you may want to try orange or another close color.

Figure 3-28. *The duplicated block cluster from the green "if" block, with some values changed so it can be applied to yellow tape*

The code for having the mBot follow the heart track is now done, and you can see what the finalized code looks like in Figure 3-29. The robot will follow a line and adjust so it stays on track, then increase its speed over the green tape and decrease its speed over the yellow tape. I added a block inside the code for detecting green tape to have the mBot play a meow sound every time it passes over the green tape. There are lots of interesting changes you can make to customize your mBot. You could program the robot to stop over red tape, play sounds, or even build your own track for it.

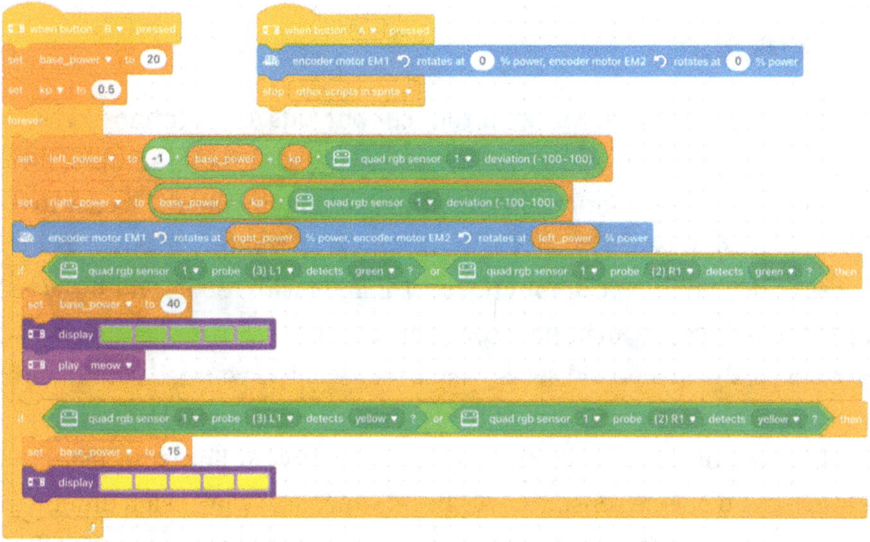

Figure 3-29. *The finalized code of the entire program with the code for both button B and button A*

Other mBot Projects

The mBot is very versatile and can be programmed for other fun projects. It has a distance sensor which can be used to program it for obstacle avoidance. It also has the CyberPi which comes with a programmable screen, and it has a microphone and speaker that can pick up your voice and play audio.

The box the mBot comes in has tutorial instructions for simple projects. I also recommend looking at some of the example programs that come with the mBlock IDE. This gives you an idea of what the mBot is capable of, and you can make changes to those programs or write your own custom program.

If you are feeling adventurous, the mBot supports Python coding inside the online mBlock IDE. This is a great way to introduce your kids to coding while using the hardware you already bought. It is also convenient since it doesn't involve setting up and installing an IDE.

Conclusion

Block coding is the best way to introduce your kids to programming. It doesn't require much typing, but it also teaches basic programming logic. The block coding platform also encourages creativity since it is easy to drag in silly code blocks like making your mBot play a "meow" sound every time it sees a specific color. Combining block coding with robots will show your kids that their code can impact something in the real world. For kids who love Legos, the Makerzoid set is great because it lets your kids build and program their creations. The mBot is another great project because first you have to build it, then you can program it to follow lines and see colors. It also has a distance sensor and CyberPi which lets you design other types of programs for it. In Chapter 4, we will learn how to write code in Python using the micro:bit and a Raspberry Pi!

CHAPTER 4

Youth Coding Projects

Learning how to code isn't as hard as it looks, especially if it is fun. In this chapter, we will introduce your kids to learning how to code in Python, and the projects are good for kids ages 14–18. Traditionally, schools will teach coding by lecturing about variables or asking you to create programs for sorting integers. We are going to skip over all the boring stuff and teach your kids how to code their very own games. By inspiring your kids that coding is fun, they will want to do more in the future!

The micro:bit is a small programmable board loaded with sensors and LEDs which is easy to take with you on the go. It also skips over all the annoying IDE setup by letting you program in the browser. Your kids will also learn how to use a Raspberry Pi which is a powerful minicomputer and a favorite for both educational use and hobbyists alike!

Micro:bit

For beginning programmers, the micro:bit is one of the best learning devices. It supports both block coding and full Python programming. This makes the micro:bit good for any age and skill level, so if your kid is a little too young for Python, you can still keep the device and have them learn block coding with it. There is also almost no setup required. You just plug up the micro:bit to your computer's power, go to the website, and start coding!

© Cassandra Chin 2025
C. Chin, *Raising Young Coders*, https://doi.org/10.1007/979-8-8688-1393-1_4

The micro:bit is more interactive than traditional coding since all your code gets sent to something physical. The board is packed with a lot of sensors which gives you many options for programming. It comes with 25 LED lights, two buttons, one touch button, an accelerometer, a microphone, a speaker, a radio, a light, a temperature sensor, a compass, and several pins. The only downside to the micro:bit is the limits on what you can do with the LEDs, but that just makes it ideal for learning because it encourages your kids to experiment with all the sensors.

- Age range: 9–16

- Difficulty: Intermediate

- Amount of time: 1 afternoon

- Learning outcomes: Write your first Python code, learn how sensors work (accelerometer, buttons, LEDs)

- Materials needed:

    - Micro:bit GO Starter Kit

    - A computer with a web browser and USB slot

Purchasing Advice and Assembly

When purchasing your micro:bit, there are a lot of different sellers and different bundles that they try to sell with the device. I recommend buying the micro:bit GO Starter Kit which can be seen in Figure 4-1 and is micro:bit's official kit that comes with a micro:bit, battery holder, two AAA batteries, and USB. The cable lets you upload your code to your micro:bit using a wired connection, and the battery pack is great if you want to take your micro:bit with you to show a friend.

Figure 4-1. *This is the micro:bit kit that comes with a battery pack*

To assemble your micro:bit, first put the two batteries into the battery pack. The battery pack has a white connector at the end of its cable. That goes to the top-left corner behind the micro:bit, which is your battery connector. Now that the micro:bit has power from the battery, we still need to plug the micro:bit into the computer so that we can upload code to it later. Find your USB cable from the kit and plug it into the micro USB slot on the micro:bit, then plug the other end into your computer. Finally, to turn your micro:bit on, the power button is on the back in between the two cables you just plugged in.

Drawing Your Own Pixel Art Image

Now that our hardware is set up, we now need to open the website for our IDE where we will do all the coding. We will be using the MicroPython website at this link: `https://python.microbit.org/`. **Do not** use the micro:bit mobile app. The app only supports MakeCode Python which won't be compatible with the instructions in this book.

We will be using MicroPython, not to be confused with MakeCode Python. MicroPython is written in Python 3, and it allows you to use external Python libraries. MakeCode Python has crippled functionality since it was written to complement the MakeCode Block editor and is written in static TypeScript. Overall, MicroPython is better for Python coding, and MakeCode Python is better for block coding.

Our first project is to draw a pixel art image which will be displayed on the 5x5 micro:bit LED screen. In the future, we will call functions on the image to move it, but for now, we are just going to draw the image on the display.

Figure 4-2. *This is the MicroPython editor when you first open it. The center is for the coding area where you'll be at most, the left bar is for reference, and the right side is a simulation of the micro:bit*

When you first land on the `https://python.microbit.org` website, you will see some starter code that's shown in Figure 4-2. Lines that start with "#" are comments which will be ignored by the program. Delete everything under "while True:" since we will be writing our own code. After deleting your starter code, it should look something like this:

```
from microbit import *
while True:
```

Now we need to create a new "image" variable that will hold the pixel art drawing we create. To create a new variable, the syntax is `image = Image()`. But then we need to tell the program exactly what our image will look like. You can see in the code below the numbers are in a 5x5 array which matches the micro:bit board. Follow the same syntax but draw your own, unique image!

The image I created will draw out a slime with bright shiny eyes. Each number represents the brightness of each LED light. The value 0 is for no light, and 9 is the brightest. I recommend drawing out your image with 0 for nothing and 5 for your drawing. Then go back and add a 9 value where you want to put an eye or a detail. Some ideas for images are a slime, a duck, a dog, or create your own!

Remember to tell the program to display your image on the board. Below where you define your image variable, you will need to code in `display.show(image)`. This tells the program to show the "image" variable you just created onto the micro:bit. Listing 4-1 shows the completed code that will draw a cute slime and show it on the micro:bit.

Listing 4-1. Code to draw a slime and display it on the micro:bit with the code you need to add highlighted in bold

```
from microbit import *
image = Image('00500:'
              '05050:'
              '59095:'
```

```
                '50005:'
                '05550')
display.show(image)
while True:
```

The last step is to upload your code to your micro:bit. Connect your micro:bit to your computer using a USB cable. Then click the "Send to micro:bit" button at the bottom of the code editor and click through the tutorial prompts. You will get a prompt that says "python.microbit.org wants to connect." If your device is properly plugged in, it will see it as "BBC micro:bit." Select the micro:bit device and connect it. The image you drew should now be displayed on the 5x5 LED screen like in Figure 4-3. Feel free to modify the code until you like your image. Remember to upload your code with "Send to micro:bit" every time you make a change.

Figure 4-3. *The micro:bit is lit up in the pattern of a slime. The eyes are twice the brightness compared to the body. You can draw any picture you want on the micro:bit!*

If your code doesn't compile, it will send an unhappy smiley to your micro:bit. The most common mistake in Python is getting the tabs and spacing right. When you define your image variable, also remember to put ' marks around each line break. The editor will let you know which part of your code is broken by highlighting it with a red squiggly.

Rolling the Image

We are going to use the built-in accelerometer to detect motion and make your pixel art image roll to the edge of the screen when you tilt the micro:bit. First, you are going to program your image to move one pixel down when you tilt your micro:bit down.

You will put your first line of code under while True:. First, press "tab" on your keyboard, then type if accelerometer.was_gesture('up'):. This lets the micro:bit know that it should do something when it gets tilted down. The up and down is flipped on the accelerometer, so that's why we are calling it up rather than down.

Then on the next line, press "tab" on your keyboard again which is required for Python syntax. To shift the image down, type display. show(image.shift_down(1)). This calls a method that will shift the entire image down by one pixel. Upload your code to your micro:bit and tilt the board up to see what happens! Here is the code:

```
while True:
    if accelerometer.was_gesture('up'):
        display.show(image.shift_down(1))
```

Next, we will program the image to roll down. The code is very similar except now we reverse the up and down words. The code is also stackable; don't delete your previous code, just add a couple of lines to make it look like this:

```
while True:
if accelerometer.was_gesture('up'):
        display.show(image.shift_down(1))
 if accelerometer.was_gesture('down'):
        display.show(image.shift_up(1))
```

Remember to save your work in the bottom-right corner. Upload your code to the micro:bit and run it. The image can now roll up and down but not left and right. We are going to program the image to roll left first. Since we have two spare buttons on the micro:bit, we are also going to program the "a" button to tilt the image left as well. By using an "or" operator, we can tell the micro:bit to listen to both motion and the button press.

The next line needs a tab, then type `display.show(image.shift_left(1))`. This tells the image to shift left by one pixel. If you want the image to shift left more than one pixel, you can modify the "1" value to be a different number.

We are also going to program some sound effects when the image rolls. On the next line after `display.show(image.shift_left(1))`, put a line of code for `audio.play(Sound.SLIDE)`. Your code should look like this:

```
if accelerometer.was_gesture('left') or button_a.was_pressed():
        display.show(image.shift_left(1))
        audio.play(Sound.SLIDE)
```

Upload your code to your micro:bit and test for when you press the "a" button and when you tilt the board left. You should see the image shift and hear the "Slide" sound effect.

If you want the full list of sound effects, find the reference tab on the left bar. Then look for the "Sound" category, and you'll find all the available sounds under "Select tune."

Now we are going to program the image to roll to the right. Put your code right underneath the last block of code. The first line's "if" statement is similar, but this time we need to check for "right" and whether "b" button was pressed. In the second line, change it to shift right rather than left. For the third line, we will play the same "Slide" sound effect:

```
if accelerometer.was_gesture('right') or button_b.was_pressed():
    display.show(image.shift_right(1))
    audio.play(Sound.SLIDE)
```

Listing 4-2 shows what your code should look like so far with the code you added in this section highlighted in bold. We now have a fully rolling image that tilts in all four directions. Feel free to add sound effects to the up and down gestures. I have made the slime yawn when it moves down and make a happy sound when it jumps up. Remember to save your work!

Listing 4-2. This will display the slime on the micro:bit and roll it in all four tilt directions.

```
from microbit import *
image = Image('00500:'
              '05050:'
              '59095:'
              '50005:'
              '05550')
display.show(image)
```

CHAPTER 4   YOUTH CODING PROJECTS

```
while True:
    if accelerometer.was_gesture('up'):
        display.show(image.shift_down(1))
        audio.play(Sound.YAWN)
    if accelerometer.was_gesture('down'):
        display.show(image.shift_up(1))
        audio.play(Sound.HAPPY)
    if accelerometer.was_gesture('left') or button_a.was_
pressed():
        display.show(image.shift_left(1))
        audio.play(Sound.SLIDE)
    if accelerometer.was_gesture('right') or button_b.was_
pressed():
        display.show(image.shift_right(1))
        audio.play(Sound.SLIDE)
```

Jumping Sky High

In the next part, we are going to teach our slime or animal of choice to jump so high that it jumps off the screen. Then we will teach it to jump back down. To do this, we will need to use a for loop!

The golden logo on the micro:bit can act as a third button when you touch it, so that's what we will use to start the jump sequence. Under all your previous code, start a new if statement with if pin_logo.is_touched():. This will tell the micro:bit to do something if the golden logo is touched.

We are going to use the image.shift_up() method again to shift our image up. The problem is if we set it to image.shift_up(4), the image will teleport 4 blocks up rather than jump 4 blocks up. To solve this, we will first tell the image to shift up by 0, 1, 2, 3, and 4 a step at a time. That's a lot of steps, and it can get very tedious. So we are going to use a for loop to do the counting for us!

"For" loops are a very common programming language control structure. This is like the loyalty stamp cards you get at your favorite ice cream store. Every time you buy a scoop of ice cream, you earn one new stamp for your stamp card. After you collect 10 stamps, you get your 11th scoop of ice cream for free. This is similar to the for loop in your program because the "i" value gets incremented by one each time the loop iterates.

After `if pin_logo.is_touched():`, press enter to go to the next line, and hit "tab." Then write your "for" loop with `for i in range(5):`. This loop will create a temporary variable called "i." It then assigns i the number 0, on the next iteration 1, then 2, 3, and 4:

```
if pin_logo.is_touched():
        for i in range(5):
```

We have the "i" variable set to increment, but now we need to display our image shifting up. On the next line, hit tab and code in `display.show(image.shift_up(i))`. Rather than putting a number inside the parentheses, we put in "i" which is assigned to a number that changes each iteration. On the next line, write the following code: `sleep(500)`. This tells the loop to wait before starting the next iteration. Without this, the code will execute faster than it can display the LEDs on screen, meaning you won't see anything happen. Upload and save your code to see if it works.

```
if pin_logo.is_touched():
    for i in range(5):
        display.show(image.shift_up(i))
        sleep(500)
```

The image jumps up, but it never comes back down. We are going to teach it how to jump down by using a "for" loop which counts in the opposite direction from 4 back down to 0.

Write your second for loop with for i in range(5, -1, -1):. It should have the same tab spacing as your previous for loop. This loop will start at 5 and count down to 0, at an increment of –1. The "i" value will go through 5, 4, 3, 2, 1, and 0.

The next two lines will be the same as the previous "for" loop. We are still using image.shift_up because to bring the image down, the image is still technically above the screen. We are just telling the program to shift the image up less and less to bring it back down.

```
for i in range(5, -1, -1):
    display.show(image.shift_up(i))
    sleep(500)
```

The last step is to add some music when your image jumps up. The music library is not imported by default, so we will have to import it manually. Add in the import music line as shown here:

```
from microbit import *
import music
```

We will write our code under if in_logo.is_touched():. Hit tab once and type music.play(music.NYAN, wait=False). This will tell the micro:bit to start playing the music called NYAN. If you remove wait=False, the image won't jump until the music is done playing. But by setting the wait to false, the image will jump and play music at the same time.

After making all of these changes, your code should look the same as Listing 4-3.

If you want to play a different song, start typing "music.", then you'll get a pop-up that lists other songs you can play. If you want to look at the full documentation of the music class, find the ? mark in the bottom-right corner and click "MicroPython documentation" which will bring you to the full docs. Use the left panel and find Music.

Listing 4-3. This is the final code for the micro:bit with the code that rolls the slime and has it jump when you touch the gold logo contact highlighted in bold.

```
from microbit import *
import music
image = Image('00500:'
              '05050:'
              '59095:'
              '50005:'
              '05550')
display.show(image)
while True:
    if accelerometer.was_gesture('up'):
        display.show(image.shift_down(1))
        audio.play(Sound.YAWN)
    if accelerometer.was_gesture('down'):
        display.show(image.shift_up(1))
        audio.play(Sound.HAPPY)
    if accelerometer.was_gesture('left') or button_a.was_
    pressed():
        display.show(image.shift_left(1))
        audio.play(Sound.SLIDE)
    if accelerometer.was_gesture('right') or button_b.was_
    pressed():
        display.show(image.shift_right(1))
        audio.play(Sound.SLIDE)
    if pin_logo.is_touched():
        music.play(music.NYAN, wait=False)
        for i in range(5):
```

```
        display.show(image.shift_up(i))
        sleep(500)
    for i in range(5, -1, -1):
        display.show(image.shift_up(i))
        sleep(500)
```

What's Next

You have now finished coding your own rolling and jumping slime on the micro:bit. If you have the micro:bit with the battery pack, you can easily take it with you and show your friends and family. If you want to do more coding, you can keep modifying this program, or you can start your own project.

I recommend going through the left Reference panel to see what else you can do with your micro:bit with the sensors you have available. You can also click the Ideas tab where they have different project ideas and tutorials on how to code it. These programs give you a simple version of the program and suggest ways you can improve it. These are great starter templates if you are looking for a fun project.

If you are feeling adventurous and want a look at the in-depth MicroPython documentation, click the small "?" icon in the bottom-left corner. Then click "MicroPython documentation." This style of documentation is identical to what professional developers refer to when they are coding. The documentation will give you an in-depth explanation of every possible class and method and what it does. This is a little complicated, so I recommend looking at some of micro:bit's project ideas for inspiration on what you want to code next!

Raspberry Pi

The Raspberry Pi should be every kid's first computer. It is priced affordably and has some of the best tool kits for both educational learning and hobbyist programs. With all the smartphones and prebuilt computers, it has become increasingly difficult to understand what happens in them. The Raspberry Pi will allow your kids to build their own computer.

In this project, your kids will learn how to program paper LED fish to glow with the press of a button. They will get to draw their own fish and light them up with the LEDs. By the end of this project, your kids will have learned how to set up the Raspberry Pi hardware and operating system, wire sensors to a breadboard, and code in Python.

- Age range: 14–18

- Difficulty: Advanced

- Amount of time: 3 afternoons

- Learning outcomes: Code with Python, wire LEDs and a button on a breadboard, learn about GPIO pins

- Materials to buy:

    - Raspberry Pi 3 or higher

    - Power supply for the model of Raspberry Pi you own

        - Pi 3: 5V 2A+ (10 watt) micro USB power supply

        - Pi 4: 5.1V/3.0A DC (15 watt) via a USB-C connector

        - Pi 5: 5.1V/5.0A DC (25 watt) via a USB-C connector

- HDMI cable for the model of Raspberry Pi you own
  - Pi 3: Standard HDMI cable
  - Pi 4 and 5: Micro HDMI to HDMI cable
- Micro SD card preloaded with Raspbian (Raspberry Pi OS)
- Pi T Cobbler
- Breadboard
- ~10 breadboard wires
- 2 3-volt 5mm LED light diodes
- 1 4-pin 12mm breadboard push button (6mm will also work)
- Materials you need and may already have:
  - TV or monitor display
  - Keyboard with USB cable
  - Mouse with USB cable
- Materials for art:
  - Paper
  - Scissors
  - Coloring supplies

Buying a Raspberry Pi

For this project, you will need a Raspberry Pi 3 or higher. The Raspberry Pi 3 is priced at $35 which makes it quite affordable. The newer Raspberry Pi 5 has a faster processor and more memory, but they are double the price. We are only going to write simple Python code and wire sensors to a breadboard, so the Raspberry Pi 3 will work just as well.

The best place to buy a Raspberry Pi is from the official Raspberry Pi website at raspberrypi.com. Go to their productions section and find what model of Raspberry Pi you want (3, 4, or 5). Then click Buy Now or scroll down to find their official resellers. Select your country and find a seller that works for you.

You will also need to buy a micro SD card with Raspbian (Raspberry Pi OS) preloaded. I found it easier just to get this on Amazon or a certified reseller (`https://www.raspberrypi.com/resellers`). If you are already familiar with Raspberry Pis, it is possible to image your own micro SD card. This requires a computer and an SD card reader, along with the imaging software off the Raspberry Pi website. If you have never used a Raspberry Pi before, I recommend just buying the micro SD card with Raspbian preinstalled since it will help you start writing code quicker. For the rest of the Raspberry Pi parts like the breadboard and buttons, you can just price shop between your chosen reseller and Amazon.

Booting Up the Raspberry Pi

Getting your Raspberry Pi working is just like setting up your very own computer. The Raspberry Pi is essentially a motherboard, processor, memory, and graphics card all in one. But we still have to connect it to a display and add memory. We will be breaking up the setup into two steps: building the Raspberry Pi and setting up the operating system.

Never remove the micro SD card while the power is on. This can lead to data corruption!

The first step is to put the micro SD card into your Raspberry Pi. This is the storage that holds the operating system and all our data. The micro SD card slot is very well hidden on the back of the Raspberry Pi as seen in

Figure 4-4. When the micro SD card is plugged in, it will stick out on the short side of the board, and the front of the card will be visible when you are looking at the back side of the Raspberry Pi.

Figure 4-4. *The Raspberry Pi with HDMI and power plugged in on top, two USBs stacked on top of each other for the keyboard and mouse to the left, and the micro SD card hidden under the board to the right*

Next, we will plug the Raspberry Pi up to any display that accepts HDMI. This can be a computer monitor or the TV in the living room. Use your HDMI cable to connect it to the wide slot on the Raspberry Pi. Then connect the other end to the back of your display. Now connect your keyboard and mouse to any of the four USB slots on the Pi.

The last cable is for your power supply. On a Raspberry Pi 3, this will be a micro USB, and on a 3 or 4, it will be USB-C. Plug the cable into the slot on your Raspberry Pi, then plug the power supply into an outlet for

power. A sign that your Raspberry Pi has power is green or red lights on the board. If your monitor or TV display is not showing anything, try switching between different inputs using a TV remote or buttons around the display.

Configuring the Raspberry Pi Operating System

With your Raspberry Pi working, you should see some screens go by, then a welcome message for the Raspberry Pi Desktop. When you click Next, you will be asked to input your country and time zone. If your English isn't your native language, check "Use US Keyboard." This is important because we will be coding in Python which uses English.

Next, you will need to create a default user account as seen in Figure 4-5. This will become the default username and password you will need to type when booting up your Raspberry Pi. Choose a secure password and something you can remember. The next step is selecting a Wi-Fi network. This step is important and shouldn't be skipped because your Raspberry Pi will need it to update the operating system.

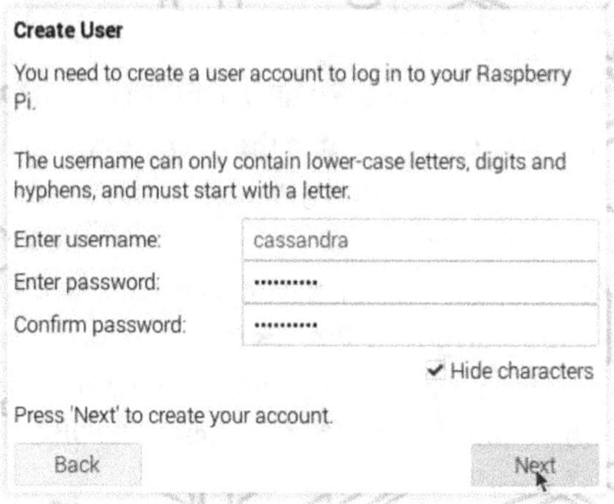

Create User

You need to create a user account to log in to your Raspberry Pi.

The username can only contain lower-case letters, digits and hyphens, and must start with a letter.

Enter username: cassandra
Enter password: ••••••••••
Confirm password: ••••••••••

                                      ✓ Hide characters

Press 'Next' to create your account.

  Back   Next

Figure 4-5. *Setting up the Raspberry Pi operating system and creating a user account*

When prompted to choose a browser, you can pick either Chromium or Firefox; both are great open source web browsers.

Finally, we get to software updates. This is especially important if you bought a micro SD card preinstalled with Raspbian since it will be several versions behind. The updates will take a few minutes, so this is a good chance to take a break. When the updates are finally finished, click the button to restart your device.

Making the LED Blink

Now that the Raspberry Pi is fully set up, we are going to start our first project which is making a single LED light blink. This is a great first exercise since it is very simple and is a good way to both learn the basics and test your hardware. To do this, first we have to wire the LED on the breadboard, then we will code it with Thonny on the Raspberry Pi. Each of the three Raspberry Pi projects builds on top of the last one, so I recommend doing them all in order.

Wiring the Breadboard

For the first LED, I chose to use a red LED light. To get our LED to light up, we have to wire it and connect it to the Raspberry Pi. We will use the Pi T Cobbler to bridge our Raspberry Pi to the breadboard where we will do all the wiring. Connect your thick Pi T Cobbler to the long slot in your Pi. One side of the cable is marked in white, and this side should be at the outer edge of your Raspberry Pi. This is a very tough connection, so I recommend having an adult do this. Then put the other end of the cable into the Pi T Cobbler board, which has a notch so it will only fit in one direction.

The Pi T Cobbler is a tool that helps divide up all the pins on the Raspberry Pi and labels them for us nicely on the breadboard. Place your Pi T Cobbler on your breadboard as shown in Figure 4-6. Be sure to line up

118

the last gold pin on the Pi T Cobbler with the last hole on the breadboard. Since we will be doing most of the wiring on the bottom, you can give yourself more space by placing it a little higher. However, the Pi T Cobbler must have contact with both the lower and upper half of the breadboard. The placement of your Pi T Cobbler is very important, so double-check it!

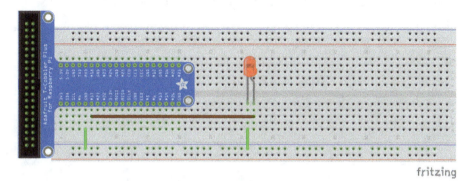

Figure 4-6. *The wiring diagram for the Blink program*

For wiring a single LED to the breadboard, you will need three wires and one LED. Follow the diagram in Figure 4-6 to know where to put the wires. The LED light can be tricky since it is directional with a short and long side. The short side is your negative and goes on the left, and the long side is positive and goes on the right.

To form a complete circuit, the LED needs to connect to both ground and power. The Pi T Cobbler and breadboard provides us with direct power and ground connections to the Raspberry Pi. The short cables help us connect to ground (labeled as GND on the cobbler) to the LED's negative. Then we have the LED's positive connected to GPIO pin 17 (labeled as #17). The GPIO pin is a programmable slot that controls the flow of power. In the next section, we will be programming the GPIO pin 17 slot to give power and remove power to control the LED's blinking.

Coding the LED with Thonny

To make our LED turn on, we will have to program it. In the Raspberry Pi OS, go to the top-left corner of the screen and click the Raspberry icon. Then hover over the Programming item and open Thonny as seen in Figure 4-7. This IDE will let us program Python code directly to the GPIO pins.

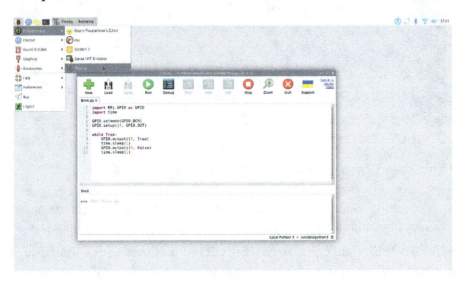

Figure 4-7. *This screenshot shows how to open Thonny and has an example of the code for the first project, Blink*

We will be writing a program named Blink which will blink the LED on and off continuously at a one-second interval. The first section of the code imports all the classes we will use. Then the program sets up the GPIO pins to tell the program which slots we will use. Finally, the "while True:" section is what the program sees and executes in a loop.

This program will output power to GPIO pin 17, do nothing for one second, turn off the power for GPIO pin 17, do nothing for one second, and then repeat. Our LED's power source is wired directly to the GPIO pin which will cause it to blink on and off slowly. You can see the full program in Listing 4-4.

120

Listing 4-4. The code for the Blink program. The LED will blink on and off continuously at a one-second interval.

```
import RPi.GPIO as GPIO
import time

GPIO.setmode(GPIO.BCM)
GPIO.setup(17, GPIO.OUT)

while True:
    GPIO.output(17, True)
    time.sleep(1)
    GPIO.output(17, False)
    time.sleep(1)
```

Save your work and name it "Blink.py" with the ".py" so that the system knows it's a Python file. Run the program and watch your LED blink! When you are done with the program, you can press the stop button to stop your LED from blinking indefinitely.

Adding a Button

A blinking LED is cool to look at, but pressing a button is more fun. In this second project, we are going to wire a button to the breadboard and program it to control the LED light. We will program it so that every time you press the button, it changes the state of the LED light.

Wiring the Button

For the wiring of the button, we are going to add more wires and a button. Leave all your previous work on the breadboard! We are going to use the same LED and wires for this project.

We are going to place the button first. The button should go toward the right of your breadboard and be placed so that it stretches across the middle like in Figure 4-8. The contacts of the button should be facing up and down. The button shown in the diagram is a 6mm breadboard button, but I am using a 12mm button since it looks a little nicer. Both buttons work and wire similarly. Just place your wires in the same vertical line as the button's contacts in your breadboard.

For the wiring, we are going to add three additional wires, making it six in total. The button needs to be wired to power, and we will control it using GPIO pin 22. This will be programmed in the next step so that when the button is pressed down, it naturally forms a complete circuit which is detected by GPIO pin 22.

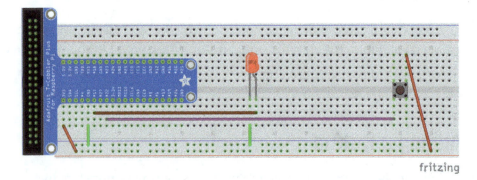

fritzing

Figure 4-8. *The wiring diagram for the ButtonPress program. This uses the same wiring as the Blink program but with three additional wires and a button*

Coding a Button Press

Now that we have finished wiring the button, we finally get to program it to work. Go back to Thonny and start a new file for your second program. If you want to copy some of your work from the previous file, the first four lines of code are exactly the same.

For the fifth line of code, we are going to set up GPIO pin 22 as an input. This tells the program to use pin 22 and listen for a current. When the button is pressed down, #22 will receive power, and when the button is not pressed, #22 won't receive power. We can program the code to do different things based on whether or not it sees power in GPIO pin 22.

Normally, to wire a button, we would have to put a physical resistor into the breadboard. But the Raspberry Pi has a built-in resistor which we can tell the button to use in code. That is why we put in pull_ up_down=GPIO.PUD_DOWN while setting up GPIO pin 22.

The actual code which the program executes to make something happen is always under while True:. The GPIO.output(17, GPIO.input(22)) line of code will turn GPIO pin 17 (mapped to the LED) on or off based on the state of GPIO pin 22 (mapped to the button). This means that every time the button is pressed, it sends a signal to pin 22. Then we use code to tell pin 17 to send a signal to turn the LED on. The final line of code is a sleep which will prevent the code from triggering too often because of button stuttering. You can see the finished code for ButtonPress in Listing 4-5.

Listing 4-5. The code for the ButtonPress program. The LED will turn on while the button is pressed down.

```
import RPi.GPIO as GPIO
import time

GPIO.setmode(GPIO.BCM)
GPIO.setup(17, GPIO.OUT)
GPIO.setup(22, GPIO.IN, pull_up_down=GPIO.PUD_DOWN)

while True:
    GPIO.output(17, GPIO.input(22))
    time.sleep(0.05)
```

Save your work as a separate file from the first program and name it "ButtonPress.py." Now run your program and press the button! You'll notice that while you are holding the button, the LED will be on, and when you let go, it turns off. In the next section, we will teach you how to keep the LEDs on using variables.

Catching Fish

We are finally at the last project for the Raspberry Pi. We will program and design two LED paper fish to turn on and off interchangeably at the press of a button. This project may look complicated, but you already have most of the wiring and code done from the previous two projects.

Wiring Fish

To control two fish, we will need two LED lights. We already have one LED light wired from the previous two projects, so we only need to add one additional LED. We will also have to add two more breadboard wires. For the second LED light, I chose to use a blue LED. The second LED will be wired to share the same ground connection as the first LED, and its power source will be connected to GPIO pin 27. You can see the wiring diagram below in Figure 4-9.

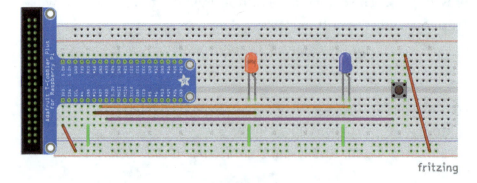

Figure 4-9. The wiring diagram for the CatchingFish program. It is the same wiring as the ButtonPress program but with an additional LED and two breadboard wires

Finally, it is time for a little art project! We are going to turn our LEDs into glowing paper fish like Dr Seuss's red fish, blue fish. Draw and color two fish on a piece of paper; they should each be about one inch long. Then cut out your paper fish. To make the fish fit on the LED lights, we will need to cut a small slit in the middle of the paper. The easiest way to do this is by folding the paper in half and making a small cut in the middle. Then place it on the LED as seen in Figure 4-10. You don't have to just draw fish. You can draw a butterfly, flower, or come up with your own ideas!

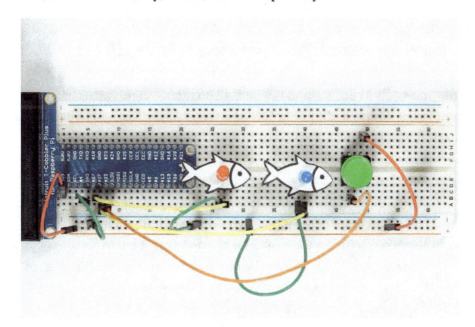

Figure 4-10. *Two paper LED fish wired onto the breadboard*

Coding Fish

Now it is time to program our LED fish. Start a new project in Thonny and name it CatchingFish. Feel free to copy the first five lines of code from your previous ButtonPress program.

We will need to add an additional GPIO setup line for setting up GPIO pin 27 which our new, second LED uses. Then define the variables, led = True and button = False, which we will call upon in the while True: block.

You can think of a variable as writing down a note on a piece of paper. The note will have a title so that you can find it easily later which is the variable name. The variable data is what you write down in the note. We use this to save the state of the LED, so we remember whether it is on or off. This makes it easy to flip the LED on and off.

The while True: section is where all our active code will execute to control the button and LEDs. We will be using an if statement to determine that if the button just got pressed, it should light up the LED. However, rather than directly telling the LEDs to light up, we will be changing the state of the led variable to True or False.

Next, we need to turn our LEDS on or off by applying our variables to the GPIO pins. We set GPIO pin 17 to the value of LED where True is on and False is off. To make the two LEDs alternate, we need to set the second LED connected to GPIO pin 27 to be opposite by putting a not in front of the "led" variable. The last line of code is a sleep so that the code waits 0.05 seconds before repeating. You can see the fully completed code for the CatchingFish Python program in Listing 4-6.

Listing 4-6. The final Raspberry Pi code for the CatchingFish program. The two LEDs will invertedly turn on and off each time the button is pressed.

```
import RPi.GPIO as GPIO
import time

GPIO.setmode(GPIO.BCM)
GPIO.setup(17, GPIO.OUT)
```

```
GPIO.setup(27, GPIO.OUT)
GPIO.setup(22, GPIO.IN, pull_up_down=GPIO.PUD_DOWN)

led = True
button = False

while True:
    if (not button and GPIO.input(22)):
        led = not led
    button = GPIO.input(22)
    GPIO.output(17, led)
    GPIO.output(27, not led)
    time.sleep(0.05)
```

Save your work and run the program. Each time you press the button, the LED fish will alternate which one is on or off. The LEDs remember their state because we programmed a variable.

You have now completed the CatchingFish program! The fish are caught when they light up. No matter how fast you click the button, you can't catch both fish at the same time. But maybe there is a solution if you modify the program to allow you to catch both fish. Give it a try, and see what other interesting changes you can make to the program!

Exploring with the Raspberry Pi

The Raspberry Pi is a great multipurpose educational computer. If you are looking for more activities to try, you can download recommended software off the Pi. To find the menu item, click the Raspberry in the top-left corner, go to "Preferences," then click "Recommended Software." The best educational software will be in the "Programming" category. They have programs like Scratch block coding, Greenfoot for early Java learners, Visual Studio Code which professional developers use, and more.

The Raspberry Pi also has one of the largest hobbyist and educational communities. There are countless online tutorials for different projects to try. It is compatible with a whole range of sensors, making it possible to build your own robot, use it as a house security camera, or even build a retro arcade system.

You and your kid now have your very own Raspberry Pi minicomputer and the basic knowledge of how to use it. This is only the start of your kid's educational journey with the Raspberry Pi!

Conclusion

The best way to teach our kids how to code is by inspiring them with fun games and projects. The micro:bit lets you skip over the usual IDE setup, and it will quickly bring your code to life with their portable board. The Raspberry Pi is a great first computer, and your kids can learn how to program their own LED paper fish to light up by wiring a button to a breadboard. Having fun first-time coding projects will give your kids a positive experience and inspire them to want to do more in the future. In the next chapter, you will learn how it's important for your kids to have positive role models, and I will introduce you to some stories from successful women in technology.

CHAPTER 5

Five Women in Tech Role Models

For this chapter, I interviewed five role models who are modern, successful female technologists. It is important for kids to have good role models because it influences whether they want to pursue technology. From a young age, I was fortunate to get to know some female technologists. I saw them do a lot of fun projects like creating demos for 3D printers and Lego robots. By having relatable role models, it has inspired me to pursue technology so that I can do something cool like them. I wish to share these stories of how these women were inspired to pursue technology in hopes that it inspires you and your kids as well.

All the women had one thing in common. They had many positive influences while growing up which inspired their passion for technology. There are many different forums that positive influences can take. Gaming is one of the biggest ones not only because it is fun, but many games encourage getting your friends involved. Some games like *Minecraft* even encourage modding and coding which has inspired thousands or millions of kids to pursue technology.

© Cassandra Chin 2025
C. Chin, *Raising Young Coders*, https://doi.org/10.1007/979-8-8688-1393-1_5

Spending time with your kids can be one of the largest positive influences for them. With busy schedules and daily necessities, it can be hard to find time with your kids. Kids highly value the moments when you listen to them and take an interest in their hobbies. The projects in this book are fun for both parent and child which makes it a good hobby to do together. This creates a positive influence on your kids since it associates doing technology with time with you.

Computer science is not just a career option anymore, it is the starting point for entering almost every industry. When we are looking at traditional career choices, we may think of the doctor, lawyer, banker, etc. However, in each of these careers, there is a need for code. I have a friend whose parents aren't doctors, but they are still in the medical industry since they write code for medical equipment. Even for lawyers, it is beneficial to learn coding since the number of tech start-up companies that need legal assistance just increases every year. Coding has become just the entry point for many careers that you wouldn't want your kids to miss out on!

Kaitlyn Hornbuckle

Kaitlyn Hornbuckle is currently studying computer science with a focus in cybersecurity and digital communication arts at Oregon State University. As a published student writer with the College of Science at OSU, she inspires the next generation by interviewing scientists and writing technical articles such as how professionals are leveraging artificial intelligence to revolutionize the life sciences industry. As a course development intern, she also assists in editing online textbooks at Lumen Learning, an education technology company that designs accessible courseware adopted by numerous US colleges and universities.

Since graduating from high school, she has dedicated the past six years to improving technology education for young learners. Kaitlyn served as an instructor for a Kids Day Workshop at KubeCon Salt Lake City to demonstrate how Java programming can be fun, especially when it comes to Minecraft. She was also the Director of Technology with Lavner Education, leading small teams, teaching courses, developing tutorials, and conducting research on a variety of STEM topics to make a difference in a fast-paced environment, one student at a time.

Kaitlyn has a strong passion for teaching technology to both kids and peers alike and is invested in a technology career path. Computers were never her go-to career, but she has experienced many positive influences showing how technology can be fun, and now she wants to share that with others.

Kaitlyn's parents gave her access to a computer when she was just three years old. Having full access to her own computer from a very young age has helped her to discover how technology is fun with her family and friends. She would also use iMovie to create short murder mystery videos with her friends, then post-process them together by adding effects. Together they would show their videos to their families and improve them based on feedback.

Gaming has played a big role in inspiring Kaitlyn's passion for technology. Her favorite activity is playing *Minecraft* with her friends. Kaitlyn and her friends wanted to play a *Minecraft* mod called Pixelmon together which meant they had to learn how to set it up. In order to get the mod working on her laptop, it took a few days to troubleshoot the performance, and she learned how to read crash logs. After solving the problem for herself, she helped her friends out, and they got to play the game together. *Minecraft* has been a great way for Kaitlyn to learn technology since it allowed her to play with her friends, and there are a lot of fun mods and add-ons that encouraged her to learn technology.

In high school, Kaitlyn started a 3D modeling club, and this was when she discovered her passion for teaching. During her time at the club, she learned how to do 3D modeling with online tutorials and helped her club members when they got stuck. She found that teaching others was a huge motivator since she had to always be a half step ahead to teach them. During this time, her mom also introduced her to an event called Devoxx4Kids where she taught the kids how to 3D model a shark using Blender with one of her club members. Kaitlyn found that teaching technology to others is fun, and she learns a lot herself while she does it.

While Kaitlyn was working on her computer science and cybersecurity degree, she taught many technology classes to kids over the school year. Kaitlyn taught the kids how to do *Minecraft* 3D modeling, Roblox game design, Python coding, and even developed some courses herself. Through this experience, she was both improving her technical skills and learning how to teach technology to others.

Kaitlyn learned that when teaching kids technology, she had to avoid using tech jargon (or technology terms that we take for granted). Coding concepts aren't that difficult to learn, but it is easy to lose the kids' attention if you use words they don't understand. Rather than assigning "variables" values, she would describe to the kids that she is putting a number in a box. When put into words the kids can understand, they will listen and learn very quickly.

One lesson she learned during her teaching experience was keeping a positive attitude even during failure. Kaitlyn was working with a student to program a fish to fall from the sky in a Roblox game. It took them a couple of hours after class to figure out the fish was spawning in the wrong location. Whenever their code wouldn't work, Kaitlyn knew that the student would get demotivated if she showed her own frustration, so she positively redirected the student's attention to solving the problem together. When the code finally worked, the student's happiness was priceless. Through this experience, she learned that when teaching others, it is important to stay positive, and failure is just an opportunity to brainstorm alternative solutions.

Kaitlyn's passion for technology today is because she experienced how it can be fun while growing up. She never knew she wanted to go into technology, but through games and teaching others, she saw the potential technology had and how it would connect her with others.

Ixchel

Ixchel Ruiz has developed software applications and tools since 2000. Her research interests include Java, dynamic languages, client-side technologies, and testing. Java Champion, Oracle ACE pro, Testcontainers Community Champion, CDF Ambassador, Hackergarten enthusiast, open source advocate, public speaker, and mentor.

Ixchel has always had a strong passion and interest in technology while growing up. However, she wouldn't call herself a child genius, and she didn't magically fall in love with computers. Ixchel's dad played a strong influence in her life by involving his daughter in his technology projects, showing her how it works, and letting her help.

One of the projects that Ixchel remembers most fondly is when her dad was designing a satellite dish. Back before there was cable television, television would receive signals and channels through a satellite dish which is mounted on the house's roof. Ixchel's dad was redesigning the shape of the satellite dish to receive signals more efficiently while not expending as much energy.

Although designing a satellite dish may seem like a complicated adult project, there are still many ways Ixchel's dad included her. The satellite dish had many layers of fiberglass, and each layer needed to be polished. Ixchel was able to help by polishing some of the layers of the satellite dish. The important part is that she wasn't just helping her dad with extra hands. While she helped her dad, he would explain how technology works like why the satellite dish needed so many layers or how the dish itself operates. It was treated more as a learning opportunity for Ixchel, and moments like this are what sparked and engaged her interest in technology.

Growing up she has always been encouraged to keep an open mind, where no question is considered stupid. Her dad would ask her, "Hey Ixchel, why do you think the sky is blue?" Her honest answer was that she didn't know. But this opened an opportunity for discussion where she could ask questions like this, which challenge how the world already works and why things are like this.

In high school, Ixchel joined a computer lab where they built an array of LEDs and then programmed them. Through this experience, Ixchel learned that she actually enjoyed programming a lot. She felt that programming lets you do more with a smaller set of tools, and you don't burn yourself from touching the keyboard.

When it came down to deciding what degree Ixchel wanted to pursue, she was torn between electronics and communication, which is the degree her dad took, or computer science where she did some programming in high school. Ixchel kept an open mind and took the third path which is taking both degrees, and today she is more of a programmer. Ixchel never magically took an interest in computers; instead, it was positive influences like her dad that helped to develop her passion for technology.

Kat Cosgrove

Kat is a Lead Developer Advocate focused on the growth and nurturing of open source through authentic contribution. In particular, her specialties are approachable 101-level content and deep dives on the history of technology, with a focus on DevOps and cloud native. She has been involved in the Kubernetes project for years, in particular the Kubernetes Release Team. She was the release lead for v1.30 Uwubernetes and currently serves as a Release Team subproject owner and SIG Docs tech lead.

Kat's passion for technology didn't happen overnight; her interest in computers started when she was very young. When Kat was a child, their family had a shared Windows 98 desktop in the living room. Both she and her younger brother wanted a computer, so the parents were fair to both kids and gave each of them an individual computer. Kat received hers for her ninth birthday, and it has become part of her life ever since.

Having access to a full computer at a young age has had the most influence on Kat's love for technology. She always enjoyed playing video games on the SNES console she had at home. But at the time, there were some games that she couldn't buy because they were only sold in Japan. With her computer, she learned how to install a SNES emulator, so she could play games she wouldn't normally have access to like the *Sailor*

Moon fighter games. Installing an emulator at the time required her to learn about how file systems worked and networking. There are still a variety of game emulators being developed today which can be a fun way to learn technology.

Kat also had some experience building her own fan website using Geocities for a couple of her favorite characters from *Gundam Wing*. To build her own website, she bought some books to learn about HTML and CSS code. This also became a good way for her to interact with her dad because he would help her with building her website when she got stuck. Geocities is a thing of the past, but websites today are still built using programming languages like HTML, so it can be fun to build a website about something you are passionate about.

A lot of games today have a strong modding community that encourages players to write their own code for fan-made content. Kat has had experience with games like *Baldur's Gate 3*, *Skyrim*, and *Fallout* where users are actively coding new game content and sharing it with each other. Just being able to download and install a mod requires some computer proficiency, but there are a lot of video tutorials that can be a good learning experience. Much of the younger generation of kids today (myself included) learned technology by modding *Minecraft*, which is fun to do with your kids!

Following Kat's passion for anime and video games, she also enjoys cosplaying. It has been increasingly common to combine technology with cosplay to create different lighting effects throughout the costume. Kat had a project where she used an Arduino to control lighting and sound effects in a prop gun. It was a simple mechanism where the gun would light up and make a sound when she pulled the trigger, but she still had to learn how to code the Arduino board to make this happen. Cosplay costumes are similar to Halloween costumes, and it can be a fun project to program your own costume with lighting effects.

Kat's passion for technology really started when she received her first computer. After having a computer, she found a lot of fun projects to try and to do what she wanted to; she had to learn some coding or computer skills. But these skills are universal, and when you learn them once, you can apply them to something else. As a kid, Kat had found fun ways to learn coding which inspired her to become the technologist she is today.

Joanna Lee

Joanna Lee is the Vice President of Strategic Programs and Legal at CNCF and the Linux Foundation, where she manages strategic programs that are designed to support the health, growth, and sustainability of open source ecosystems. Joanna also oversees legal and policy initiatives, governance, and code of conduct incident response. Prior to joining the Linux Foundation and CNCF, Joanna served as a legal and strategic advisor to open source software foundations, tech standard-setting organizations, and a broad range of technology companies.

Technology has become so widespread that even nontechnical occupations are now involved in technology. Joanna is a lawyer who has always had a strong passion for technology since she learned about it in college. Technology is exciting to her because it is always changing. For an injury attorney or a tax attorney, the laws don't need to change that often, but with technology and AI today, the laws have to match the speed of technology innovation.

In Joanna's early career, she found herself working with a lot of technology start-ups. The founders of these companies are very smart since they designed and developed their own products, but they may not have business or legal sense. Start-ups require a lot of funding, so Joanna would help them to write up the legal documents between the company and their investors. She also would provide them with general advice like how to provide their employees with their pay and stock options. To do all this, she had to learn about the company's products which required learning about their technologies. Through this experience, she was working closely with technology companies and had to be open to learning about technology.

With generative AI becoming more and more common, it presents some legal challenges. Before gen AI, when a developer writes code or an artist draws a picture, it is obvious that it is their own work. However, it has become the industry's standard for developers to use an AI assistive tool like Copilot to help them write code. These AI models are trained off of lots of code which may be copyrighted, then use this data to generate their own code. It is then put into question whether it is legal to use this code in an open source project which is free to use for all. There is no authoritative answer, but Joanna has created recommendations for the cloud-native community of developers like checking the terms and conditions of AI tools, responsibly using AI as an assistive tool, and keeping in mind what kind of content developers are producing.

Joanna also helps open source foundations with drafting Code of Conduct documentation. Open source communities work together to write code and contribute it to projects, but sometimes people can get toxic online. Code of Conduct is essentially a set of rules for a project that encourages people to treat each other with respect. This also helps the respectful treatment of women and minorities so that their voices get heard on these projects regardless of who they are.

One area where Joanna is particularly passionate about is helping developers protect themselves against patent trolls. These companies make money by threatening technology adopters with lawsuits. But many of these claims are frivolous and can be avoided if you are armed with the right knowledge. Joanna has created a program with the CNCF to raise awareness and protect developers against false patents. She has also created an illustrated picture book to help explain patent trolls in a fun way. Defending against patent trolls is just one of the ways that she helps the developer community with her legal expertise and love for technology.

It used to be that only programmers ever learned or touched technology, but that is not the case anymore. Joanna has a strong passion for technology and is able to help the technology community with her legal expertise. It will only become more and more important for everyone to learn tech, especially with advancements like artificial intelligence.

Emily Fox

Emily Fox is a DevOps enthusiast, security unicorn, and advocate for Women in Technology. She promotes the cross-pollination of development and security practices. She has worked in security for over 14 years to drive a cultural change where security is unobstructive, natural, and accessible to everyone. Her technical interests include containerization, least privilege, automation, and promoting women in technology. She holds a BS in information systems and an MS in cybersecurity.

Serving on the Cloud Native Computing Foundation's (CNCF) Technical Oversight Committee (TOC) from 2022 to present and as chair of the TOC 2023–present and co-chair for KubeCon+CloudNativeCon China 2021, Europe 2022, North America 2022, Europe 2023, and CloudNativeSecurityCon 2023. She is also serving as the vice chair of the Confidential Computing Consortium's Governing Board. She is involved in a variety of open source communities and activities and is currently focused on accelerating Zero Trust, enhancing security for AI, driving crypto-agility in a post-quantum world, and commoditizing confidential computing technologies.

Today, Emily is a professional software engineer, but that wasn't something she imagined she would be doing. As a student, Emily was a little bit of a rebellious child and saw her parents doing technology for the Navy, so naturally she decided she would do something else. As a high school student, Emily always had an interest in art. She enjoyed fine art and sculpture. Emily wanted to combine her passions with her career, so she took a Fine Arts degree in college.

When Emily first got into her first job, she thought she could be creative with her work and take pride in it. However, she found that art as a hobby is very different than art as a job. When Emily worked with clients, her art would get critiqued, she didn't always agree with her clients, and there were very harsh deadlines to meet. This endless cycle of being judged for her own artistic work took a mental toll on Emily's health, and she knew she had to change careers.

After Emily had turned in her resignation notice, it was her mom who encouraged her pursuit of a technology career. The new job was at a computer science company where she was doing some basic desk work. At this job, Emily saw that she could do more if she learned how to code. So, she went back and earned her information systems and cybersecurity degrees while juggling the job and raising two young kids.

Emily felt that software development allowed her more flexibility regarding where she could show her artistic creativity. She had her day job where she would develop and deploy software for customers, later finding even great community and creativity by contributing to open source projects and efforts by sharing her own ideas.

Open source lets you write code and make changes, even for day-to-day things. One project she is currently involved with is a project to convert her custom cooking recipes into open source code. Not only versioning her recipes as she makes tweaks and changes, but it lets her convert imperial to metric units or make recipe substitutions automatically. She is also exploring how to build a simple database of flowers and other plants to help her plan her garden and link to those recipes at harvest time. Although Emily originally started with art, her real artistic creativity shows with technology.

Next Steps for You and Your Child

Thank you for reading this book. I hope you and your kids have learned a lot from some of the projects in this book. The best way to get your kids into technology is by inspiring them that technology is fun so that they will decide by themselves that they want to do it in the future. It is also important to inspire our daughters since they are equally capable of learning technology and deserve the opportunity. Technology is a growing industry that extends into almost every other industry. This is only the start of your child's journey through technology!

If you enjoyed this book or have projects that you've already completed with your child, then please share it with your friends and family. Especially if you know someone who has a daughter, this opportunity could be a life changer for them!

Index

A

Artificial intelligence (AI), 8, 10, 131, 139–141

B

Bar chart, school subjects kids, 14, 15
Block coding, 63
  crab dance, 71
  crab move, 68–70
Block programming, 63

C

Cloud Native Computing Foundation's (CNCF), 138, 140, 141
Code of Conduct, 138, 140
Coding, 1, 16, 63, 130, 133, 137, 138
Color Sorting Machine, 78
Computer science, 2, 3, 8, 10, 13–16, 130, 135, 142
Computer scientist, 16
Copilot, 139
Cosgrove, K., 136–138
Crocodile, 78
CyberPi, 79, 87, 97, 98

D

Desktop computer, 3, 4
Developer conference, 10
Devoxx4Kids, 18, 132
Distance sensor, 66, 71–75, 79, 97
Dropbox, 11
Dual Motor Lunar Rover, 79

E

Educational software, 6, 127

F

Female software engineers, 11
Female technologists (role models), 129
  Cosgrove, K., 136–138
  Fox, E., 141–143
  Hornbuckle, K., 131–133
  Lee, J., 138–140
  Ruiz, I., 134–135
For loops, 109
Fox, E., 141–143
Friendly slimes project
  bending LED lights, 45–46
  blue slime building
    facial features, 34–35

GPSR Compliance
The European Union's (EU) General Product Safety Regulation (GPSR) is a set
of rules that requires consumer products to be safe and our obligations to
ensure this.

If you have any concerns about our products, you can contact us on

ProductSafety@springernature.com

In case Publisher is established outside the EU, the EU authorized
representative is:

Springer Nature Customer Service Center GmbH
Europaplatz 3
69115 Heidelberg, Germany

www.ingramcontent.com/pod-product-compliance
Lightning Source LLC
LaVergne TN
LVHW051640050326
832903LV00022B/828

*9 7 9 8 8 6 8 8 1 3 9 2 4 *